WISDOM OF THE WORD

Bible Study Series

Revelation

Vision of Hope and Promise
Part 2

Marie Coody

Linda Shaw

Helen Silvey

Jeannie McCullough, Executive Editor

BEACON HILL PRESS

OF KANSAS CITY

ISBN-13: 978-0-8341-1827-0
ISBN-10: 0-8341-1827-0

Printed in the United States of America

Cover Design: Darlene Filley

All Scripture quotations not otherwise designated are from the *New American Standard Bible*® (NASB®), © copyright The Lockman Foundation 1960, 1962, 1963, 1968, 1971, 1972, 1973, 1975, 1977, 1995. Used by permission.

Permission to quote from the following additional copyrighted versions of the Bible is acknowledged with appreciation:

The *Amplified Bible, Old Testament* (AMP.), copyright © 1965, 1987 by The Zondervan Corporation.

The *Holy Bible, New International Version*® (NIV®). Copyright © 1973, 1978, 1984 by International Bible Society. Used by permission of Zondervan Publishing House. All rights reserved.

The *Holy Bible, New Living Translation* (NLT), copyright © 1996. Used by permission of Tyndale House Publishers, Inc., Wheaton, IL 60189.

The *Living Bible* (TLB), © 1971. Used by permission of Tyndale House Publishers, Inc., Wheaton, IL 60189. All rights reserved.

The *Message* (TM). Copyright © 1993. Used by permission of NavPress Publishing Group.

Scripture quotations marked KJV are from the King James Version.

Library of Congress Cataloging-in-Publication Data

Coody, Marie, 1925-
  Revelation : vision of hope and promise / Marie Coody, Linda Shaw, Helen Silvey.
    p. cm.—(Wisdom of the Word Bible study series ; 3)
  Contents: Pt. 1. Lessons 1-11.—Pt. 2. Lessons 12-22.
  ISBN 0-8341-1792-4 (pb : pt. 1)—ISBN 0-8341-1827-0 (pb : pt. 2)
    1. Bible. N.T. Revelation—Textbooks. I. Shaw, Linda, 1951- II. Silvey, Helen, 1931- III. Title. IV. Series.

BS2825.5 .C66 2000
228'.0071—dc21
                                       00-039850

10   9   8   7   6   5   4   3   2

Contents

About Wisdom of the Word

Wisdom of the Word (W.O.W.) was founded in 1986 by Jeannie McCullough in Bethany, Oklahoma. It began as a weekly Bible study at Bethany First Church of the Nazarene. In the first year the study grew to over 400 members, and women from other churches and the community began joining. The local enrollment of Wisdom of the Word eventually exceeded 1,000 and has included men, women, and children of all ages and many denominations. Wisdom of the Word has been an instrument in uniting the community of believers as well as reaching the unchurched and the lost. It is now ministering to thousands through videos and cassette tapes and other programs such as Children of the Word, prison ministries, and missions.

About the Name

W.O.W. began as "Women of the Word." Then when men began to join in the study with the women, Jeannie changed the name to Wisdom of the Word, not only to retain the W.O.W. acronym, but also because it reflects the mission:

> To have our lives visibly changed by gaining wisdom from God's Word and responding in radical obedience to His voice.

About Jeannie McCullough

Jeannie McCullough is a pastor's wife, mother, and grandmother. Her life and ministry have taken her to Bethany, Oklahoma, where her husband, Mel, is the senior pastor at Bethany First Church of the Nazarene. She understands firsthand how radical obedience to God's Word can change a life.

Southern Nazarene University granted Jeannie an honorary doctorate in 1997. Due to her humor and honesty as well as her unique insights and application of the Scriptures in daily living, she is in great demand as a speaker throughout North America. Jeannie strives to be a "salt tablet" who will make others thirsty for God's Word. As she has committed herself to being a student of the Word, God has given her many opportunities to share what He is teaching her.

About the Authors

This is the third study presented by Wisdom of the Word. A team of three writers joined together to write lessons for this particular study:

• LINDA SHAW was the solo writer for the first W.O.W. study book on the Book of Ezra. She is the mother of Jonathan, Jenny, and Daniel. Linda is a licensed clinical social worker and began the W.O.W. prison ministry at a women's prison in the Oklahoma City area.

• MARIE COODY has been an integral part of the W.O.W. study since its beginning in 1986. She and her husband, Darwyn, have two grown daughters and are enjoying retirement.

• HELEN SILVEY is from a family of writers. She is a widow with four grown children. Helen has been a group leader for W.O.W. for many years and is very active in the life of Bethany First Church of the Nazarene.

Interested in starting a W.O.W. Bible study?

If you are interested in starting a W.O.W. Bible study, attending a study in your area, or ordering additional materials, please contact the W.O.W. outreach office in Bethany, Oklahoma, at 405-491-6274.

Introduction to Revelation

The Book of Revelation, *the revelation of Jesus Christ* (1:1), was written by John to the seven churches in Asia (modern-day Turkey) (verse 4). Some controversy has arisen concerning the identity of John, but he probably was the beloved apostle, son of Zebedee and brother of James. The Early Church fathers almost unanimously agreed that he was the author, and tradition throughout history has affirmed this belief. The language and the many allusions to the Old Testament make it almost certain that the author was a Palestinian Jew writing in Greek but thinking in Hebrew, steeped in Temple and synagogue ritual, and very familiar with the Old Testament.

While John was in exile on the Isle of Patmos for preaching the gospel of Christ he was told to write in a book the things he was to see in a vision, and to send it to the seven churches. Bible scholars disagree over the date Revelation was written, but most believe it was between A.D. 90 and 95.

The emperor of the Roman world at that time was Domitian, who demanded public worship of himself as lord and god. Prior to this, Christians had suffered persecution under Rome but mostly had been considered as a sect of seditious Jews, and much of the persecution had been at the hands of the synagogue and priests. Now Christians were confronted with a choice: Caesar (Domitian) or Christ. Once a year, everyone in the empire had to appear before the magistrates, burn incense to Caesar, and say, "Caesar is Lord." To address him in speech or writing required one to begin, "Lord and God." Refusing to call Domitian "Lord" and give him worship was considered an act of political disloyalty. The refusal of Christians to obey resulted in the second great wave of persecution against the Church. Christians were subjected to public ridicule, economic boycott, imprisonment, exile, even death. Revelation was written to comfort and strengthen them.

The Book of Revelation gets its name from the Greek word "apocalypse," which is translated "revelation" and literally means "an unveiling"—taking away that which obscures. Apocalyptic literature is a recognized style most common to the time between the Old and New Testaments but also frequently found in the Old Testament and in the first century A.D. It is called apocalyptic because it reveals truth expressed in symbolic and guarded language. Revelation is a Christian apocalypse, and its meanings were meant to be understood by these first-century congregations. The symbolism found in Revelation would have been very familiar to a people acquainted with Old Testament and apocalyptic writings.

The primary purpose of apocalyptic literature was to reveal the mysteries of God to believers experiencing oppression and suffering and to reassure them that despite the evil in this world, God will be the final Victor. A glimpse is given of the rewards of eternal life in heaven for all who overcome and remain faithful. Dark pessimism might be the theme on one page, only to be followed on the next page by a sudden, glorious breakthrough of God's power and might. This style of writing with its sharp, bold contrasts, drawing upon familiar symbols to speak about spiritual realities, was familiar to the people of the first century. Symbols are important as a way of understanding something difficult to explain or draw in a picture. One example is found in Revelation 17:5-6. Evil is difficult to explain, but *THE MOTHER OF HARLOTS AND OF THE ABOMINATIONS OF THE EARTH . . . drunk with the blood of the saints* paints with words a graphic description.

As you begin each day, use this acrostic to help you study:

Wait for the Holy Spirit to teach you as you read His Word.

Obey what God instructs you to do.

Remember to praise God for insights and promises fulfilled.

Discover for yourself the incredible faithfulness of God!

Revelation is also prophecy (1:3; 22:7, 18-19). Prophetic writing is even more common in Jewish and Christian literature than in apocalyptic literature. Prophecy contains an evangelistic and ethical message that intends to call people to repentance. Its meaning is not as mysterious or hidden as the apocalyptic; it has clarity and immediacy. It affirms God's will to us here and now with a cutting edge. It emphasizes our freedom in making decisions before God. It also predicts future events.

The use of numbers is very pronounced in Revelation, with 1, 3, 4, 7, and 12 being the favorites. The number 7 was used more than 50 times. Seven is the number of perfection, indicating completion and showing all things are accomplished according to God's plan.

Revelation is not plural; it is singular—one revealing vision. This revelation came from God, through Jesus Christ, to the angel, to John, to the churches, and to us. It deals with problems in seven first-century churches, problems representative of the Church in every age, everywhere. The *Expositor's Bible Commentary* refers to Revelation as a "unique source of Christian teaching and one of timeless reverence" and as the "most profound and moving teaching on Christian doctrine and discipleship found anywhere in Holy Scripture." Through Revelation, God seeks to lead us into authentic Christian discipleship by explaining Christian suffering in the light of how Jesus' death bought us victory over evil, and telling us of the ultimate end of evil and final victory of the Lamb of God and His followers. The language of Revelation describes the reality of the conflict between the sovereignty of Christ and the satanic power of which Paul warns us in Ephesians 6:12.

Revelation is about many things—power, battles, freedom, faith, evil, hope, and warnings—but it has one great theme: Jesus Christ, the Son of Man in the midst of the churches in this present age, Judge and King in the dispensation to come, and the Lamb rejected yet someday to reign in glory on the throne, no longer meek and humble but with absolute power and control. The Gospels tell of Christ in His humiliation and death; Revelation reveals Christ in His majesty and glory.

Revelation also has a strong emphasis on worship, both on earth and in heaven. It also begins and ends with a special promise of blessing for obedient readers (1:3; 22:7) and ends with a warning and curse for those who would tamper with it in any way (22:18-19).

This letter to the churches gives pastoral advice and spiritual counsel to help them resolve the problems threatening them spiritually. It is the written substitute for the work of a pastor. It seeks to define the presence and active participation of a good and sovereign Lord God in the midst of persecution, human misery, and social injustice. It was written for real believers struggling with real problems that threaten their faith. It is a call for repentance for the life and faith of every congregation of every age. Crises confront every generation of believers forming a community of faith who bear witness for God in a secular and materialistic world and face the temptation to compromise. And it reminds us that God rules above the ages and will accomplish His purpose in this age and the age to come.

Revelation is a difficult book but is definitely worth studying; you may learn to love it. If it is a hard book to understand, it is also a hard book to put down. Try not to begin your study of Revelation with preconceived ideas, but allow the Holy Spirit to teach you what God wants to say. Revelation is a book of warning, but for the faithful, obedient Christian, it is a book of glorious hope. Turn to Revelation when things seem darkest; God is in control, and "beyond the terror [is] the glory, and above the raging of men [is] the power of God" (William Barclay, *Daily Study Bible Series*).

Written by Helen Silvey

Revelation

■ **A Study of Revelation 12**

DAY ONE

The Woman— Israel

Read all of Revelation 12 aloud. Review verses 1-2.

Beginning in chapter 12, before the *seven bowl judgments* and after the *seven trumpet judgments*, John witnesses several *great signs* that reveal the true nature of the conflict between God and Satan. The vision is signaling a momentous event in God's redemption of His people.

1. A sign appeared in heaven. Write a complete description of the sign.

A sign is defined as "that which points to something else." In this portion of John's prophetic vision, the woman represents the nation of Israel.

2. How do these Scriptures explain God's relationship to Israel?

    Deuteronomy 7:6

    1 Peter 2:9

The woman's crown of 12 stars refers to the 12 tribes of Israel. The woman represents the nation of Israel and is seen crying in the pain of labor awaiting the birth of her child.

In the Old Testament, Israel is the name given to the descendants of Jacob and to the grouping of people in the 12 tribes coming from Jacob's sons. They constitute the people of God, for He chose them as His own. Scripture clearly states that Christ came to earth to establish His heavenly kingdom as a substitute for the Jewish kingdom that had failed.

3. Summarize Matthew 21:43.

God, in His grace, opens the door to salvation by faith to all people regardless of their race or tradition.

4. Record Luke 13:29.

The woman symbolizes the faithful people of God from whom and for whom the Messiah is born. She represents a people identified by their distinctive spirituality rather than their nationality.

MEMORY CHALLENGE

Psalm 103:12

As far as the east is from the west, so far has He removed our transgressions from us.

The Dragon— Satan

Read Revelation 12:3-4.

1. The second sign that John saw in heaven was a _____ that had _____ heads with _____ horns and _____ diadems.

2. In what activities was the enormous red dragon involved?

3. What is the clearest example of the existence of Satan that you are aware of today?

4. How are you experiencing spiritual warfare in your life this week?

5. Summarize the Abrahamic covenant in Genesis 12:1-3.

The mission of Israel (the woman in verse 1) was to bear the Messiah's seed to fruition. Because of the promise in the Abrahamic covenant, the Jewish people throughout history have been a primary object of Satan's attack. Satan's ruling passion is to exterminate the Jews; he knows the first great promise and prophecy in Scripture was the promise that the Seed (Jesus) would crush the serpent's (Satan's) head (Genesis 3:15). Satan's first large-scale attempt to exterminate the Jews was made by Pharaoh before God brought the Israelites out of Egypt (Exodus 1—15). God called Moses to lead the Israelites away from Pharaoh, speaking through the mysterious burning bush in the desert where Moses was shepherding sheep. The bush spoke to Moses, flamed, and burned but was not consumed. The bush has been said to be a symbol of Israel, which has not been destroyed despite the constant hatred by her enemies and their attempts to eradicate all Jews. Jews today are the purest-blooded and proudest-descended people in the world. Israel cannot be exterminated or assimilated into other nations. She is a burning bush among the nations of the world.

6. Does this give you a clearer understanding of anti-Semitism? During World War II, Hitler was responsible for killing millions of Jews in German death camps. How could this have been ignored by the rest of the world?

The dragon had 7 heads, 10 horns, and 7 diadems (crowns) representing his power and the kingdoms of the world over which he rules. The stars that plunged to earth with him are generally considered to be the angels who fell with Satan and became his demons.

Read Ezekiel 28:12-19 (NIV). Satan was not created evil. Ezekiel is quoting a description of Satan given to him by *the Sovereign LORD* (verse 12, NIV). He was once *anointed as a guardian cherub*, God says, *for so I ordained you* (verse 14, NIV). He was perfect in intellect and perfect in form. He was *in Eden, the garden of God* (verse 13, NIV) and had a special place of prominence in guarding the throne of God. Suddenly we watch that perfection come crashing down.

7. Isaiah 14:12-15 looks deeper into the nature of Satan's rebellion. List the five vows he speaks in his heart.

   I will:

   (1)

   (2)

   (3)

   (4)

   (5)

Satan's sin above all was pride, and pride goes before destruction (verse 15). He was created with freedom to choose his course, just as we are. He used his choices against God, and God allowed his choices, just as He allows ours. All of us are growing either in likeness to God or in likeness to the devil.

The current fascination with Satan and demons is alarming. Christians must beware of excessive gullibility, as well as extreme oversimplification. Knowledge about Satan and evil angels alerts Christians to the danger and subtlety of satanic temptation. We should not become too absorbed in satanic forces. Satan and demonic forces are active, but they are limited. They are mighty, but they are not almighty. Satan is a created being who can tempt but not force. He and his demonic forces have been overcome by the life, death, and resurrection of Jesus Christ. This victory ensured that countless numbers would be delivered from the dominion of darkness and transferred to the kingdom of Christ (Colossians 1:13).

MEMORY CHALLENGE

Is there the slightest doubt that all of your sins have been removed?

The Son—Our Savior, Our Refuge

Read Revelation 12:5-6.

The woman identified as Israel in verses 1 and 2 is said, in verse 5, to give birth to a son, a male child.

1. What is the destiny of her son?

2. Read the prophecy of:

    Psalm 2:7-9 and record verse 9.

    Micah 5:2, 4 and record verse 4.

Against the gods of pagan mythology and the Gnostics' speculations (claims of superior secret spiritual knowledge), John wrote in agreement with the messianic expectations of Old Testament prophecy. The Messiah was born to rule all the nations with an iron scepter (with strict justice). Although it was a time of worldwide blessing and prosperity, it was also a time when sin was still rampant.

3. What did God do to miraculously preserve the mission and ministry of the Messiah (Revelation 12:5)?

4. How had God prepared to care for the woman?

Scriptures recording the birth of Jesus Christ bring thoughts of Christmas—Mary, Joseph, Jesus in a manger, the star, angels singing, the shepherds, the wise men, gifts. Thoughts of Satan are the opposite of "Joy to the World" and "O Come, Let Us Adore Him." In John's vision there is no joy or peace on earth. John saw a dark, invisible scheme of the powers of hell planning to destroy Israel's Son, Jesus. Satan knows that Jesus will ultimately destroy

him. In reality, Christmas is a celebration of victory over Satan. Spiritual warfare raged against bringing Jesus to earth to become the sacrifice for all who will believe in Him. With Jesus now sitting at the right hand of God in heaven, Satan focuses his wrath on those who have accepted God's message of salvation and know Him as Messiah and Savior. The son of the woman was rescued to the throne of God, and the woman fled into the wilderness, where God had prepared a place for her.

5. What picture comes to your mind when you think of the woman in the wilderness?

Biblical examples of people fleeing for safety:

God cared for the Israelites for 40 years while they journeyed from the slavery of the Egyptians to the Promised Land of Canaan.

Elijah escaped to the brook Cherith where he was fed bread and meat by ravens (1 Kings 17:1-7).

Fleeing for his life from Jezebel, Elijah was fed by an angel of the Lord (1 Kings 19:1-8).

God told Mary and Joseph to flee to Egypt to protect Jesus from being killed by Herod (Matthew 2:13).

Our strongest place of refuge is in God who always welcomes us and provides care for us.

6. Read Psalm 37:37-40 and list the benefits the righteous receive from taking refuge in God.

7. Keeping in mind that the geography of Israel featured high mountains and deep rifts (clefts, caves), name some images of God that describe His loving care of us.

All of us need places of refuge in the storms of life. There are times when we are physically exhausted and emotionally struggling with hearts that are broken from hurts, disappointments, and grief. We often have people who stand by us with comfort, support, and encouragement—a smile, a phone call, a letter, or a flower. These things may not be so significant when we are strong but can lift us and give us hope in our down times.

Just as we need a place of refuge, we need to be that place of refuge for others. That is the blessing of godly love and compassion. Synonyms for places of refuge and shelter are sanctuary, haven, harbor, shield, safeguard, and protection from danger and trouble. God has always created places of refuge for His people, as indicated in Revelation 12:6 and 14.

8. What places of refuge, both physical and spiritual, has God supplied for you in the midst of trouble?

The dictionaries do not list "family" as a synonym for a place of refuge and shelter, but our homes and families should be places of security and safety.

Faye Gandy and her home are places of refuge for her family. As the oldest of five children, Faye became the mother figure after her parents' early deaths. She was married and had four children. Her husband died when their children were in mid-high, high school, and college. As a licensed X-ray technician, she provided for her children, including their college educations.

Holidays for her children and their families, plus her siblings and their families, meant gathering in Faye's home. She insisted they stay with her—no motels were allowed. The first arrivals slept on beds, then there were sleeper sofas, air mattresses, pallets—and in later years, bunk beds in the motor home. She prepared food weeks in advance that could be stored in the freezer so she could be ready for her family.

Faye's 80th birthday was celebrated with 150 family members (18 of them staying in her home) and friends giving loving tribute and recalling humorous incidents. Grandchildren, nieces, and nephews told of the stability that she had provided for their lives with her unconditional love and acceptance. Her love, joy, peace, kindness, gentleness, self-control, generosity, hospitality, and resilience helped establish confidence and self-worth in their lives. Her godly walk with the Lord inspired them to accept Jesus Christ as Savior and Guide. Her service as organist for her church for many years was their example of Christian service. In troubled and painful times she was a dependable listener and counselor. When disharmony came to families, she maintained contact with everyone involved. She never allowed differences to separate anyone from her love and concern. Her family and friends know she is available for them. She is a living example of the power of love and sacrifice that inspires others to want to live their lives creating the same refuge in their homes as they establish their own families.

This example of sacrificial living is not a popular concept today, but it is a powerful one for influencing the lives of others, and it will continue in the lives of those who follow us. As we accept all who come to us as sent by Jesus, silently the work of the Holy Spirit is done. Generously coming back to us will be His countless blessings.

9. Summarize Luke 6:38.

10. From these psalms select the words and phrases relating to refuge and shelter:

Psalm 57:1

Psalm 59:16

Psalm 61:3-4

Psalm 62:1-2

Psalm 63:7-8

Using the phrases you have written, pray a prayer seeing yourself receiving God's shelter and refuge. Include those for whom you are a shelter for the storms of their lives.

MEMORY CHALLENGE

Fill in the blanks:

As far as the _____ is from the _____,
so far has He _____ our
_____ from us.

Psalm 103:12

Angels

Read Revelation 12:7-9.

1. What is happening in heaven?

2. Who is fighting?

3. Who is Michael? From these scriptures, record the phrase identifying Michael:

   Daniel 10:13

   Daniel 10:21

   Daniel 12:1

   Jude 9

4. Who won the war between Michael and the dragon?

5. Paul may be referring to Michael's voice on the day of the Lord's second coming. Read 1 Thessalonians 4:16-17. Record verse 16.

6. What is the response of your heart when you read that Jesus is coming and believers will be caught up in the clouds with Him?

Michael serves as the guardian of God's people Israel. In Jude 9 he is called *Michael the archangel.* The title "archangel" means the angel who is "first, principal, chief." Only Michael is given that title in Scripture. While Gabriel is generally involved in announcing and preaching, Michael is more involved in protecting and fighting. Any power Michael has is from God. Regardless of the great battles Michael wins, or whatever great things any angels do, our only praise must go to the Lord *who alone works wonders* (Psalm 72:18).

Michael, the great archangel, and his angels force the dragon and his angels out of heaven and hurl them to earth. Michael and his angels may, even now, be fighting our battles here on earth more than we know. *Our struggle is not [entirely] against flesh and blood* (Ephesians 6:12). The outcome may depend, far more than we realize, on the armies of the invisible world.

Individual angels seem to have their special gifts and responsibilities, just as members of the Body of Christ do.

Five duties of angels:

(1) Warriors: The angels that fight with Michael in heaven against the dragon and his angels have been and are today warriors for God, emphasizing His power and authority.

7. Record phrases from these scriptures explaining the angel's responsibility:

   Genesis 3:24

   Isaiah 37:36

(2) Deliverers, Protectors: God sends His angels as deliverers and protectors of His people.

An angel of the Lord outlined step by step what Joshua and the armies of Israel must do to bring to pass the victory God had already ordained over Jericho (Joshua 5:13—6:5).

8. While David is protected from the soldiers of King Saul, he sings his faith in God's protection. Record Psalm 34:7.

9. Read Daniel 3:24-25. Record 3:25.

Other examples of protection and deliverance are:

Daniel 6:19-22

God sent His angel to shut the mouths of the lions.

Acts 12:11

The Lord sent His angel to rescue Peter from prison.

(3) Guides: Angels guide with clear and specific instructions from God.

Genesis 16:7-9: Hagar, servant of Sarai and mother of Abraham's child Ishmael, is commanded by an angel to *go back to your mistress and submit to her* (verse 9, NIV).

Genesis 19:15-17: After two angels rushed Lot, his wife, and his daughters from Sodom, one of the angels commanded, *Don't look back, and don't stop anywhere in the plain! Flee to the mountains or you will be swept away!* (verse 17, NIV).

Genesis 31:1-13: God's angel speaks to Jacob, *Leave this land at once and go back to your native land* (verse 13, NIV).

Matthew 1:20: In his dream an angel of the Lord appears and says, *Joseph son of David, do not be afraid to take Mary home as your wife, because what is conceived in her is from the Holy Spirit* (verse 20, NIV).

(4) Comforters: With encouragement and strength in their hands and voices, angels minister to God's people.

Genesis 21:14-19: An angel appears to Hagar and tells her to not be afraid.

Daniel 10:4-19: Michael tells Daniel he was there in response to his prayers, though he had to overcome demonic opposition on the way. The angel touched Daniel and restored his strength.

Matthew 4:10-11: Angels ministered to Jesus after the temptation of Satan.

(5) Messengers: Angels reveal the will of God and announce key events.

Judges 13:1-5: An angel of the Lord tells Manoah, *You are sterile and childless, but you are going to conceive and have a son* (verse 3, NIV).

Matthew 28:1-7: A white-robed angel is sitting on a stone when two women approach a tomb in Jerusalem, *Do not be afraid; for I know that you are looking for Jesus who has been crucified. He is not here, for He has risen, just as He said* (verses 5-6).

Luke 1:26-31: Gabriel says, *Do not be afraid, Mary, you have found favor with God. You will be with child and give birth to a son, and you are to give him the name Jesus* (verses 30-31, NIV).

Luke 2:9-12: An angel has appeared and the glory of the Lord lights up the sky and the hill where the shepherds tend their sheep. *Do not be afraid*, the angel says. *I bring you good news of great joy which will be for all the people; for today in the city of David there has been born to you a Savior, who is Christ the Lord* (verses 10-11).

As wonderful as the presence of an angel might be, God has given us something better. He has given His children the greatest gift of all—His presence through the Holy Spirit and in His Word. If an angel never makes himself known to us, we can still know that if one is needed in our lives, God has dispatched one to us and will continue to do so as long as we are on earth.

10.   Record Hebrews 13:2.

Suddenly, in the 1990s, angels began to be talked about everywhere. In every store something could be seen with an angel on it—books, magazines, lamps, writing pens, stationery, jewelry, kitchen plaques, and so forth. Probably no major theological issue has received as much secular attention in modern times as the doctrine of angels in the 1990s. In many minds, angels have become a mysterious and fascinating reality whereas once they were considered merely myths. What does this mean? Is it good or bad?

As we open our hearts and minds to spiritual truths, we become more susceptible to spirituality's dark side. Scripture warns us that *Satan disguises himself as an angel of light* (2 Corinthians 11:14). In Matthew 24:24, Jesus warned us that even *the elect* will be misled. Satan can be using people's fascination with angels to destroy their desire for the truths of obedience and discipline to God's Word and His gospel of grace and truth. Angels reflect a form of spirituality often centered on the personality of angels but without Jesus and God. In truth, without the commands of the Triune God, angels have no direction or power. Hebrews 1:14 describes angels as *ministering spirits sent to serve those who . . . inherit salvation* (NIV) —those who know Christ as Savior. If an unbeliever claims to have seen an angel, it is possibly one of Satan's messengers, not the Lord's. In 1 Timothy 4:1 Paul reminds us, *The Spirit clearly says that in later times some will abandon the faith and follow deceiving spirits and things taught by demons* (NIV).

Father, please convict us when we are being led astray from You!

MEMORY CHALLENGE

How far have our transgressions been removed?

Song of the Martyrs

Read Revelation 12:10-12.

1. What did a voice from heaven announce (verse 10)?

2. How did the voice from heaven refer to Satan?

3. According to the voice from heaven, how was Satan defeated?

4. What warning was sounded to the earth and sea? Why?

5. What does it mean not to love your life even to death?

In these verses we hear the song of the glorified martyrs when Satan was cast out of heaven. We are shown a picture of what might be called the cleansing of heaven. Satan, the accuser, is cast out forever. God and His Son are now without rival in the heavenly places. It is for this reason that the martyrs in heaven sing their song of triumph.

Martyrdom in itself is a victory over Satan. The martyr has chosen to suffer rather than deny his God. Every time we choose the right when we might have chosen the wrong, every time we choose to suffer rather than be disloyal, we defeat Satan.

In the massacre of students at Columbine High School in Littleton, Colorado, Cassie Bernall became a present-day martyr. A report from the *Washington Post* stated that the victims had not been picked at random. The two gunmen were motivated by hostility and hatred, not only for racial minorities and athletes, but for Christians as well. Eight of the 13 they killed were Christians. Cassie was in the library reading her Bible when the gunman asked her if she believed in God. When she answered "yes," she was immediately killed. Cassie chose to die rather than deny her Savior and Lord.

None of us know what choices we may need to make in our future. We must be willing to choose to stand for our Lord whenever we can. We begin by resisting sins of today with firmness and boldness, yet at the same time feeling compassion and love for those who hate us and could harm us. A fellow student, Craig, said at Cassie's funeral that she was a shining light for Jesus. We can all choose to be a shining light for Him today.

6. Personalize John 12:25.

The victory of the martyrs is won through the blood of the Lamb and the word of their testimony. The Lamb, Jesus Christ, overcomes Satan because of His victory at Calvary. The redeemed have conquered by the blood of the Lamb and by the word of their testimony; meaning through their receiving the "word" testified to them and confessing it by faith. In this way the testimony passed on to them becomes the testimony made by them and then becomes saving grace for others when received in faith.

7. Record Romans 10:17.

Satan's ejection from heaven leads to an intensification of his activity on earth. There are two truths to remember concerning Satan as he leaves heaven and is thrown down to earth. First, that Satan has no place in heaven represents an important victory won for man, since Satan is no longer able to accuse man before God. This suggests that God will no longer listen to accusations against His people, for they are forgiven. Second, Satan's defeat in heaven signifies that his power has been broken in the affairs of men. Even if he does intensify his efforts to control the nations and destroy the work of God, the extent of his influence is limited. For example, he has no power over the Church, and his days are numbered (verses 13 ff.).

8. Read 1 Peter 5:8-9. Record verse 9.

Does verse 11 in today's lesson encourage you to be prepared to resist Satan, *firm in your faith?* We are in a war, but Satan does not have the last word in his attempts to defeat us. Like the martyrs, our victory is won through the blood of the Lamb and the word of our testimony. Praise God!

Quote Psalm 103:12 to someone in your discussion group.

Attacked!

Read Revelation 12:13-17.

1. What was the dragon's reaction when he saw that he was thrown down to earth?

2. Explain how the woman was protected from the dragon (serpent).

3. Summarize these verses.

   Exodus 19:4

   Deuteronomy 32:11-12

The woman is to be taken care of, though it is not said by whom. That God provides for her is important, the agent He employs is not. During this period of 42 months, the woman is secure in her hiding place and inaccessible to Satan.

4. When the dragon was unable to kill the woman, where did he redirect his destructive efforts?

5. What does this passage tell us about God's people?

6. What can you do this week to strengthen your hold on the word of your testimony?

The woman, Israel, is the mother of the Messiah and therefore of the Church: she is the symbol of all God's redeemed people. Having lost the battle in heaven, Satan now directs his attack against her. But God provides her with refuge and protection.

7. Record Matthew 16:18.

Jesus has personally given His Church this assurance. We are under His divine care. Satan cannot destroy us unless we ourselves leave our place of refuge.

Certainly natural calamities such as a flood (Revelation 12:15) cannot destroy Christ's Church. Most Bible scholars see that this particular flood comes from Satan's mouth as a flood of lies, temptations, and trials meant to lure the faithful away from the refuge of the Church and into the bondage of sin. But the earth swallows up the flood so that nothing more can be done by him. The picture well illustrates the spiritual security of believers against all that Satan can do in his attempts to destroy them.

8. Personalize 1 Corinthians 10:13.

The serpent (dragon) can injure the child (Jesus) by injuring the mother (the Church). When Paul met Christ on the Damascus road, the words of Christ to him were: *Saul, Saul, why are you persecuting Me?* (Acts 9:4).

Paul's persecution had been directed against the Church; but Jesus makes it clear that persecution of the Church is persecution of himself. When we hurt and refuse the Church of the help we could have given it, we hurt and refuse Jesus Christ of the help we could have given Him. When we serve and help the Church, we serve and help Jesus Christ himself.

The dragon's anger is directed specifically against the woman's offspring who are believers (Revelation 12:17). This is a picture that tells of the coming spread of persecution all over the Church. As John sees it in his vision, Satan is cast down to earth in one last terrible convulsion, and that convulsion is going to involve the whole family of the Church in the agony of persecution.

This means there is a spiritual battle of vast dimensions going on right now for your allegiance—for your soul. If you are not aware of this conflict or feel it does not involve you, be careful! Some people are in bondage of sin and do not realize it. Satan does not have to do battle with those who are already his. On the other hand, if you are daily trying to live for Jesus, then you know you are battling with an enemy. God will equip you for the battle (see Ephesians 6:10-18) and He *gives us the victory through our Lord Jesus Christ* (1 Corinthians 15:57).

Thank You, Father.

Written by Marie Coody

Review Psalm 103:1-12.

Revelation

LESSON 13

■ A Study of Revelation 13

The Antichrist

Read all of Revelation 13, concentrating on verses 1-2; and Daniel 7:1-8, 16-25.

Satan, the master deceiver, has always tried to counterfeit everything God has done for man. Revelation 13 introduces two additional personages, who with the dragon of chapter 12 (Satan), form an unholy trinity. This evil threesome is comprised of the dragon, the beast from the sea, and the beast from the earth, a diabolical counterfeit of the Holy Trinity—God the Father, God the Son, and God the Holy Spirit.

1. What does John see and from where does it come?

2. How is this beast described in Revelation 13:1?

3. According to Revelation 13:2, this beast *was like a
_____, his feet were like those of a
_____, and his mouth like the mouth of
a _____.*

4. Reread Daniel 7:3-6. In Daniel's vision he saw four beasts. From where did they come?

5. What animals did the first three beasts resemble?

6. Reread Daniel 7:7-8, 19-20 and write a description of the fourth beast.

The 13th chapter of Revelation makes much use of symbolism, and reputable Bible scholars present different interpretations of its meaning. This beast from the sea, a composite of the beasts in Daniel's vision, is most often referred to as Antichrist. There is not complete agreement that this will be a specific person during the time of tribulation. The term "Antichrist" is not used anywhere in the Bible to refer to a specific person. The apostle John uses the word "antichrist" to refer to anyone or any teaching that opposes Christ or denies the deity of Christ (1 John 2:18, 22; 4:3; 2 John 7). But there are many scriptures that predict that someone will arise who embodies all of the attitudes, purposes, and motives of Satan and who will be used by Satan to try to defeat Christ and His followers. He is called Antichrist because he opposes everything Christ represents.

7. Read 2 Thessalonians 2:1-10. What does 2 Thessalonians 2:3 tell us must occur before the day of the Lord?

In his vision, John sees the beast coming up out of the sea, which some Bible commentators see as the sea of unrepentant humanity (Isaiah 57:20), or it may symbolize the abyss, or bottomless pit spoken of in Revelation 9:1; 17:8; and 20:1-3. Most commentators believe it means that he will come from the sea of people around the Mediterranean Sea. Tim LaHaye, in *Revelation—Illustrated and Made Plain,* suggests that the Antichrist is the "little horn" that came out of the four Grecian horns, signaling that he will be part Greek. Daniel 9:26 refers to him as the prince of the people that shall

---

Psalm 103:13

*Just as a father has compassion
on his children, so the LORD has
compassion on those who fear Him.*

come, meaning that he will be of the royal lineage of the race that destroyed Jerusalem. Historically, this was the Roman Empire. Daniel 11:36-37 tells us that he regards not "the God of his fathers" (KJV). This suggests that he will be a Jew . . . [but] will keep his Jewish ancestry a secret. . . . the Bible teaches that he will be a Roman-Grecian Jew, a composite man representing the peoples of the earth.[1]

Over the centuries, many persons have been thought by some to be the Antichrist. Whoever he is will be revealed according to God's plan and His timing, and speculation serves no purpose. What is important is that the one who abides in Christ and His Word apparently will recognize him (Revelation 13:18), and we have been given warning so that we might be prepared and strong in our faith in Christ Jesus.

8. Antichrist has been given many names in Scripture. Revelation 13 calls him a beast. By what names and adjectives do the following verses refer to him?

   Daniel 8:23

   Daniel 9:26

   2 Thessalonians 2:3 (2)

9. The beast from the sea is very similar in appearance to the dragon (Revelation 12:3). He receives his power, his authority, and his throne from the dragon, who dominates him. Record the description of his conduct as found in 2 Thessalonians 2:4:

The spirit of antichrist in the world is growing rapidly stronger and more powerful. Rebellion against law, order, morality, and honesty is rampant. Persecution of Christians is increasing throughout the world, including the United States. The stage is being set for the appearance of Antichrist. If you are not a follower of Christ, you are a part of the spirit of antichrist. Christ said, *He who is not with Me is against Me* (Luke 11:23). Are you able to sing with the blood-washed redeemed of the Lord?

I have decided to follow Jesus . . . No turning back.
The world behind me, the cross before me . . . No turning
   back.
Tho' none go with me, still I will follow . . .
No turning back, no turning back.

—Anonymous

DAY TWO

An Awesome God

Read Revelation 13:3-5.

1. Describe what John saw regarding one of the seven heads of the sea beast.

2. What was the result?

3. Who gave the beast his authority?

4. How long was the beast given to act?

Satan, the great red dragon, will stage a resurrection of the beast from the sea from what appears to be a mortal wound, a blasphemous counterfeit of the death and resurrection of Jesus Christ. This will amaze and fool the world, causing people to follow the beast and worship the dragon. This false messiah and counterfeit of Christ will receive a wound to one of its seven heads, perhaps a wound that normally would be fatal and is healed by Satan, or which will appear fatal. This will set the stage for his "resurrection," his new life, and greater authority. In Revelation 17:8, the angel tells John that the beast he saw *was, and is not, and is about to come up out of the abyss.* This leads some commentators to believe this may be an actual death and resurrection, if God grants Satan temporary power to raise the dead.

Humanity has always looked for a visible god to worship. Even as God was giving Moses the Ten Commandments on Mount Sinai, the Israelites were worshiping a golden calf at the foot of the mountain (Exodus 32). Many religions today worship inanimate statues. Christianity is unique; we worship a resurrected, living Lord. This "resurrection" of Antichrist will neutralize the powerful message of the risen and exalted Christ and will deceive the whole earth.

Will people be so easily fooled and manipulated? In the 20th century millions have followed Hitler, Mussolini, Hirohito, Stalin, and others. Sun Myung Moon declared himself to be a god and has thousands of devoted followers. Perhaps the best example in recent history is Mao Tsetung, who, in the words of John Phillips, transformed a billion Chinese "into dutiful, obedient puppets. Mao was a living god. His thoughts became the creed of his people. The little red book of his sayings was the bible of a quarter of the earth's inhabitants."[1]

None of these evil persons can begin to compare with the charisma, deceit, power, and influence of this beast whose authority comes from Satan. He will seem invincible. Only the believer, abiding in Christ and in God's Word, will have the spiritual resources to resist and worship God and Jesus Christ rather than the beast. Do you set aside a "tent of time" each day to be alone with the Lord, to listen to His quiet voice and meditate on His Word?

Revelation 13 may seem discouraging, even depressing, but take heart! We serve an awesome God—omniscient, omnipotent, and omnipresent, yet loving, merciful, and compassionate. The beast may seem invincible, but God is in control! The beast's authority will be limited to a short period of time—just three and a half years. Even the remaining time and power given to Satan is limited to what God allows. If you are a follower of Christ, you have the assurance that *greater is He who is in you than he who is in the world* (1 John 4:4).

5. Read Isaiah 40 and rejoice in the greatness of God. Write a brief prayer of praise for His greatness.

6. Summarize Revelation 3:10.

Have you *kept [His] word, and . . . not denied [His] name* (Revelation 3:8)? If Christ comes to take His Church from the world before the Tribulation, the faithful believers will not need to endure this evil; they will be with Christ Jesus. If Jesus should tarry and His Church remain here, He has promised that He will keep you.

7. Read Psalm 27:1, 3, 5, 14. Write a one-sentence summary of what these verses mean to you.
    Though all the peoples walk
    Each in the name of his god,
    As for [me], [I] will walk
    In the name of the LORD [my] God forever and ever.
    —Micah 4:5

MEMORY CHALLENGE

With what is the compassion of the Lord compared?

DAY THREE

Commitment

Read Revelation 13:5-10.

1. What came forth from the mouth that was given to the beast?

2. What else was given to him?

3. Who will worship the beast?

4. What admonition given in the letters to the churches (Revelation 2—3) is repeated here?

The dragon (Satan) gave the beast a mouth from which spewed forth *arrogant words and blasphemies . . . against God [and] . . . His name and . . . those who dwell in heaven.* Arrogance and blasphemy also characterize the little horn of the fourth beast in Daniel's vision (Daniel 7:8, 25).

5. Look up "blasphemy" in your dictionary or in a Bible dictionary and record the definition.

Satan has always been a blasphemer against God. Now his blasphemies are also directed at the inhabitants of heaven. Some Bible commentators believe this includes not only the angels and the saints who have died but also those on earth in whom God dwells, the believers who have their citizenship in heaven (Philippians 3:20).

For a brief period of time, the beast will be given the power and authority to successfully defeat and conquer the people of God. Believers will face hostility, persecution, and death (Daniel 7:21; Revelation 11:7; 12:17), but Satan and his Antichrist will not be able to overpower or destroy their faith in God and Christ Jesus. If the believer is faithful in his or her commitment and has an obedient and abiding relationship with the Lord, He will provide a clear discernment of deception and error, and the believer will not be deceived or persuaded by the power demonstrated by Satan's Antichrist.

6. What will happen to Satan and the beast after their allotted time is over? Summarize these verses to help you with your answer.

Daniel 7:26

Revelation 19:20; 20:10

During his brief time, the beast will have authority over all peoples and nations and will be worshiped by everyone except those whose names are written in the Lamb's book of life. Leon Morris believes that "John wants his little handful of persecuted Christians to see that the thing that matters is the sovereignty of God, not the power of evil."[1] This is an important truth for the Christian today and will bring strength and comfort to the persecuted believers during the Tribulation. No matter how dark and pervasive the evil around us, Satan is limited in time and authority by what the Almighty God allows.

There are many references to the book of life in Revelation. Several interpretations have been given for the phrase *everyone whose name has not been written from the foundation of the world in the book of life of the Lamb who has been slain* (Revelation 13:8). Some believe that every name was included in the book *from the foundation of the world;* the names of those who do not accept salvation are erased when they die (Revelation 17:8; see Ephesians 1:4). Others interpret the passage as *the Lamb who has been slain from the foundation of the world* (see 1 Peter 1:18-21). This rendering would mean that, from the beginning of time, God had provided for the death and resurrection of Jesus Christ that our sins might be forgiven. When we accept Christ, our names then are written in the book that registers those who belong to God. The important fact in each view is that the Lamb's book of life contains only the names of those who, by faith, have received Christ as Savior and are serving Him in obedient faithfulness.

7. What will be the final result for those whose names are not written in the book of life (Revelation 20:15)?

8. Record the words of Jesus in Matthew 10:28.

The Antichrist will establish and totally dominate a one-world government. People will follow and worship the beast because he appears invincible. In the words of the late Bishop Fulton J. Sheen (1895-1979):

> The Antichrist will come disguised as the great humanitarian. He will talk peace, prosperity, and plenty, not as a means to lead us to God, but as ends in themselves. He will explain guilt away psychologically, make men shrink in shame if their fellowmen say they are not broadminded and liberal. He will spread the lie that men will never be better until they make society better.[2]

Prophetic words, indeed! In recent years, this has become the prevailing philosophy of much of the world.

Satan has been preparing the world for a one-world government, already being advocated by godless "intellectuals" as the only solution to the problems of economic difficulties and continuous wars. Many will view the Antichrist, rather than the true Christ, as having the answer to bring peace on earth. Those without a living faith in God will be deceived!

The faithful believer in God, understanding the truth and refusing to worship the Antichrist, will be persecuted and martyred but is to respond only with perseverance and faith (Revelation 13:10; Jeremiah 15:2). The love of God can never be defended using the violence of men. Refusal to worship the beast will result in temporary suffering and death but will lead to spiritual growth and eternal life.

We will all experience dark and troubled times. It is Satan's desire that we would turn away from God when difficulties or persecutions come (Job 1:1, 9-11; 2:3-5). Instead, through patience, faithful endurance, and placing our trust in God we can use the tough times as opportunities for spiritual growth and as a witness to others of the grace of God.

If anyone has an ear, let him hear (Revelation 13:9).

MEMORY CHALLENGE

Write out Psalm 103:13.

DAY FOUR

The False Prophet

Read Revelation 13:11-12.

1. From where did the second beast come?

2. Describe the appearance and speech of the second beast.

3. What does this beast do for the first beast?

The second beast in John's vision comes not out of the sea but out of the earth. Many Bible commentators believe *the earth* to be symbolic of Palestine. This beast comes as a religious leader, a false prophet (Revelation 16:13; 19:20). He is the third person of the ungodly, counterfeit trinity, along with the dragon (Satan) and the beast from the sea (Antichrist). His function is to lead the people to worship the Antichrist, an unholy imitation of the work of the Holy Spirit in leading people to Christ.

Man has been created with a desire to worship. The Antichrist must provide an outlet for man's religious nature; he and the false prophet will create an ecumenical, world-wide church that will be so powerful it will even dominate the Antichrist during the first three and a half years of the Tribulation. This one-church false religion will serve to increase the power and dominance of the Antichrist and will be under the leadership of the false prophet.

The second beast will appear to be much more gentle than the first beast, but his gentle appearance will be deceptive. He may resemble a lamb, but he will speak as a dragon. His actions and speech will be directed by the great red dragon, Satan. He must be similar enough to the Lamb of God to entice followers of Jesus, yet at the same time, must remain loyal to his associates and dedicated to promoting the first beast. Most Bible commentators believe that when the false prophet appears he will profess to be a minister of Christ and will appear to be like Christ in meekness and humility. He will be intellectual and cultured and have a subtle cunning. Evil is greatly intensified when it is masked by a deceptive similarity to truth. Jesus warned us of this when He said, *Beware of the false prophets, who come to you in sheep's clothing, but inwardly are ravenous wolves.* Twice he emphasized, *you will know them by their fruits* (Matthew 7:15-16, 20).

4. Satan has used false prophets throughout history to deceive and seduce the people of earth. Summarize these warnings given the people of God that they might be alert and prepared.

   Matthew 24:4-5, 10-11

   Acts 20:30-31

   1 Timothy 4:1

   2 Timothy 4:3

   2 Peter 2:1-3

There are many false prophets teaching false doctrines today. Scientology and New Age movements have hundreds of followers in this country. Their spokespersons are often celebrities with great influence. We have witnessed mass suicides at the command of leaders of religious cults who claim to be prophets of God. Churches and seminaries that once proclaimed the gospel of Jesus Christ now deny His deity. A "politically correct" form of religious "tolerance" has deemed it unacceptable to believe that behaviors condemned by God are sinful, or to believe that salvation through Jesus is the only way one may come to God. The world has been prepared by Satan and will be ready to accept and believe the false prophet. People are looking for a comfortable religion that requires little or no commitment or discipline.

5. How may we recognize false prophets and/or false messages? Summarize these verses.

   Deuteronomy 18:21-22

   Romans 16:17

   1 John 4:1-3, 5-6

6. What consistent commitments are most important to guide the believer? Use these verses to help you with your answer:

Deuteronomy 13:4

Proverbs 3:5-6

Proverbs 12:15

Acts 17:11

Ephesians 4:14-15

1 Thessalonians 5:17

We must measure the truth of every message by the truth of God's Word. Seek God's guidance and direction through the study of His Word and in earnest prayer. Put your trust in God. Obey His commandments. Seek counsel from spiritual advisers who are mature in their faith, grounded and rooted in God and His Word. Mature spiritually. Flee from any messenger or message that denies that Jesus Christ is the only Son of God, that He was in the beginning with God and is God (John 1:1-2), that He was born of a virgin, suffered and died on a cruel cross for our sins, rose again on the third day, and ascended to heaven where He sits at the right hand of God, that everyone who calls on His name shall be saved (Acts 2:21-36) and that He is *the way, and the truth, and the life; no one comes to the Father but through [Him]* (John 14:6).

Have you received God's free gift of salvation through His Son, Jesus Christ? If not, take this moment to confess your sins and invite Him into your life. He is waiting and eager to come in (Revelation 3:20) and give you new and abundant life in Him here on earth and eternal life in heaven.

MEMORY CHALLENGE

Fill in the blanks:

Just as a _____ has _____ on

his _____, so the _____ has

_____ on those who _____

_____.

Psalm 103:13

Miracles

Read Revelation 13:13-15 and 2 Thessalonians 2:1-15.

1. How is the false prophet able to deceive the people?

2. What does he tell the people to do?

3. What power was given the false prophet and what was the amazing result?

4. What happens to those who do not worship the image of the beast?

Throughout Scripture we read of miracles performed to give proof of God's power, authority, and love. The false prophet uses miracles and signs to deceive men into worshiping the first beast. He *makes fire come down out of heaven* (verse 13). Once again, we see Satan imitating the works of God. Elijah called down fire from heaven in the presence of the prophets of Baal, to consume his water-soaked sacrifice to God and demonstrate God's power (1 Kings 18:17-40). Tongues of fire rested on the disciples gathered together on the Day of Pentecost (Acts 2:1-3). Revelation 11 tells of fire proceeding out of the mouths of the two witnesses and destroying anyone who tries to harm them. The healing miracles of Jesus' ministry will likely be imitated as well.

Amazed, impressed, and deceived by the miraculous signs and wonders performed by the false prophet, those who dwell on earth will obey his command to make an image of the first beast. Witch doctors, voodoo practitioners, and false religions have all used displays of supernatural demonic power to deceive and persuade the superstitious; missionaries sometimes report frightening demonstrations of demonic power. But spectacular miracles are not a reason for a believer to accept any revelation unless it is in harmony with God's Word and His revealed will. For example: God has explicitly commanded that we are not to make or worship any kind of image, idol, or god (Exodus 20:1-5). Jesus Christ gives peace and confidence before God that does not depend on supernatural displays and signs. God wants us to come to Him by faith.

5. Record Hebrews 11:6.

6. Jesus warned us against accepting false signs as coming from God. Paul also warned us to use prayerful spiritual discernment when confronted with what appear to be miracles. Forewarned is forearmed! Summarize these verses.

   Matthew 24:24-25

   2 Thessalonians 2:8-9

The false prophet will *give breath to the image of the beast, . . . that the image of the beast would even speak.* Leon Morris notes that the "breath of life" has always been associated with the Creator God and refers to the miracle as "a blasphemy exceeding that of all previous idolaters."[1] Some Bible scholars suggest that in the middle of the Tribulation, after the first beast is mortally wounded, the resurrected beast may actually be Satan indwelling the body of the Antichrist. This could explain his resurrection. Satan has always desired the worship of man (Isaiah 14:13-14), and this could also explain the increased power and dominance of the first beast at this time and the ability of the image to speak.

As in Daniel's account of the three Hebrew children (Daniel 3), those who refuse to bow down and worship this abominable image will be killed.

7. Reread 2 Thessalonians 2:1-15 and write a brief summary of what *the man of lawlessness* will do (verse 4), how it will end (verse 8), why people will believe (verses 11-12), what God has chosen us for (verse 13), and Paul's admonition to believers (verse 15).

Lord, strengthen my faith; give me spiritual wisdom and discernment that I might stand firm and hold fast to Your truth in the face of the increasing evil that surrounds us. Amen.

MEMORY CHALLENGE

On whom does the Lord have compassion?

DAY SIX

The Mark

Read Revelation 13:16-18.

1. What does the image of the beast cause to be done?

2. What does this provide?

3. What will be the number of the beast?

Before the book with seven seals was opened (Revelation 5—6), God placed His seal on His followers to protect them (7:3; 9:4; 14:1). Satan's beast now places his mark on his people. This mark protects them from the increasingly intense persecution that will be inflicted on God's followers. Everyone who accepts the mark of the beast proclaims allegiance to Satan and rebellion against God, a final decision for eternity to reject Christ. To refuse the mark commits the believer entirely to God and testifies to the world his preference to die rather than deny Christ. "So severe will be the pressure to forsake the worship of God that all normal activities of life will fall under state control."

4. Are God's people today "sealed" by God, or is this only for the Tribulation? Have you been "sealed" by God? Use these verses to help you with your answers.

   2 Corinthians 1:21-22

   Ephesians 4:30

In Revelation 13:18, we learn that during the time of the beast on earth, believers will have the wisdom and insight to be able somehow to recognize him by the *number of his name,* 666, which *is that of a man.* This knowledge will help the believer see through the evil deception of the beast. There has been much conjecture concerning the meaning of this number. Most commentators make the observation that the number seven is considered to be the complete and perfect number in the Bible, and seven is the number that represents Jesus Christ, who personifies perfection and completion. Six represents man, incomplete and falling short of perfection. The tripling of the number six indicates falling completely short and is possibly a symbolic reference to the unholy trinity. The theologian Irenaeus believed that the name of the Antichrist was deliberately concealed until the time of his appearance and warned the Church against endless speculation. He also believed that it indicates that the beast is the sum of all apostate power, a concentration of unrighteousness, wickedness, deception, blasphemy, and false prophecy.

Picture in your mind a society where nothing could be bought or sold without this mark on your forehead or hand. Your money and possessions would be worthless. You could not buy or fix food or purchase water or electricity. You could not heat or cool your home. You could flee with your family to a remote area and try to live off the land, but go no farther than one tank of gas would take you or you could flee on foot. You might choose to die a slow, painful death of starvation for yourself rather than compromise your faith, but would you have the strength to watch your children suffer? The decision to stand fast will require God-given courage and strength. Jesus encouraged His disciples to pray at all times and not to lose heart (Luke 18:1), and that is advice every believer needs to follow in any time of tribulation.

If Christ comes to take His Church before the Tribulation, the believer will escape this terrible time and will be with Him in heaven. Should the Tribulation precede the second coming of Christ, God's Word assures us that God will strengthen and comfort the believer. The eternal reward for the Christian who perseveres will be so glorious as to be beyond earthly understanding!

5. You may be going through a time of trial and/or persecution in your life. Perhaps Satan is tempting you to give up and turn away from God. God has given us many wonderful promises of His loving care for us in the midst of our times of tribulation, far too many to include in this lesson.

   Record the following verses.

   Psalm 5:12

   Psalm 9:9

   Psalm 23:4

   Isaiah 40:29

   Isaiah 41:10

The Lord is our light and salvation, our defense, our refuge, rock and fortress, our stronghold and strength, our leader and guide. He supplies power to hold fast to our faith. We need not fear nor be shaken (Psalm 27:1; 31:3-4; 46:1; 62:6). *Greater is He who is in you than he who is in the world* (1 John 4:4).

6. Jesus tells us, *Do not fear those who kill the body but are unable to kill the soul* (Matthew 10:28). Summarize these passages.

   Romans 8:35-39

   2 Corinthians 4:8-9

7. God has also given many promises of great reward for those who have endured to the end. Summarize the following verses.

   Matthew 5:10

   Romans 8:18

   2 Timothy 2:11-12

   James 1:12

   1 Peter 5:10

   These are the ones who come out of the great tribulation, and they have washed their robes and made them white in the blood of the Lamb. For this reason, they are before the throne of God; and they serve Him day and night in His temple; and He who sits on the throne will spread His tabernacle over them. They will hunger no longer, nor thirst anymore; nor will the sun beat down on them, nor any heat; for the Lamb in the center of the throne will be their shepherd, and will guide them to springs of the water of life; and God will wipe every tear from their eyes (Revelation 7:14-17).

How glorious! Praise His name! *Lord, help me and all of my loved ones endure to the end that we might kneel together before Your throne in heaven. Amen.*

Written by Helen Silvey

MEMORY CHALLENGE

On a separate sheet of paper, write out Psalm 103:1-12 from memory as much as possible.

Bible Study Series

Revelation

LESSON 14

■ **A Study of Revelation 14**

Follow the Lamb

Read Revelation 14, concentrating on verses 1-5.

1. In Revelation 13:1, where was the dragon standing?

2. Where was the Lamb standing? Who was with Him?

3. What does Mount Zion represent to those who follow the Lamb? Refer to Joel 2:32.

4. What kind of song did they sing, and who could sing it?

5. Only those who follow the Lamb could learn the song sung by the 144,000. Verses 4-5 give three other characteristics of the ones who follow the Lamb. What are they?

6. Summarize the following scriptures that explain what it means to follow the Lamb.

   Matthew 4:18-22

Mark 10:17-22

John 13:15

John 21:19-22

1 Peter 2:21

1 John 2:6

When you were a child, did you ever play a simple game called follow-the-leader? One child starts and those behind are to form a line and try to imitate exactly what the leader does. If the leader takes baby steps along a curb and then jumps high onto the grass, all that follow are to do that too. If the leader hops onto a brick wall and takes seven steps, those who follow are to do the same. Whatever the leader does, the followers are to imitate.

MEMORY CHALLENGE

Psalm 103:14

*For He Himself knows our frame;
He is mindful that we are but dust.*

25

As Revelation 14 opens, the Lamb is standing on Mount Zion with His 144,000 sealed followers. The 144,000 are the same group mentioned in Revelation 7 and bear the name of the Lamb and His Father on their foreheads. Their mark, according to author William Barclay, represents ownership, loyalty, security, dependence, and safety. They received this mark by exactly following the Lamb.[1]

Only the redeemed, the 144,000, could sing the new song; without following the Lamb, the song was unlearnable. Those loyal followers had suffered. They had experienced life and still chose to cast their lot with the Lamb no matter the consequences. They had matured and grown deep in the Lord so the song was understandable to them. They could easily learn it. To those without the mark, it was like a foreign language. They could join in the singing only if they had followed the Lamb.

The members of this sealed group bore some unique characteristics. Besides following the Lamb—which is standard fare for any believer—verse 4 tells us they had not defiled themselves with women but were chaste. What does this mean?

Commentators have many opinions about this, but there are three main ideas. The first idea is that the 144,000 are male Jews who are to serve as witnesses to the rest of the world. Either they have lost their wives in the Tribulation, have not been married, or from this point on are to live in celibacy due to their important mission. All of their energy will be taken to survive and witness during this period of history. They must take their mission very seriously and not be encumbered with a family. It is similar to the conviction that Paul held that He could serve the Lord more fully without distraction if he were unmarried.

The second possibility relates more to symbolism. In the Old Testament when Israel was evil, she was compared to an adulteress. *Their deeds will not allow them to return to their God. For a spirit of harlotry is within them, and they did not know the LORD* (Hosea 5:4). *But you trusted in your beauty and played the harlot because of your fame, and you poured out your harlotries on every passer-by who might be willing* (Ezekiel 16:15). When evil, Israel was an adulteress, but when sealed by the Lamb, the 144,000 witnesses were pure as a virgin. They represented righteousness.

The third idea compares righteousness to a virgin. In the New Testament, Christ is described as the Lamb and the Church is the bride of the Lamb. Revelation 21:9 states, *Come here, I will show you the bride, the wife of the Lamb.* Christ will only wed the pure (virgin) Church. *For I am jealous for you with a godly jealousy; for I betroth you to one husband, so that to Christ I might present you as a pure virgin* (2 Corinthians 11:2). If the 144,000 are the ones to wed Christ, they must be as pure as virgins.

This sealed group also represents the firstfruits of the har-vest. Later in this chapter we will see more harvesting, but these are the firstfruits, which were the earliest crops. They are to be set aside as the best for the Lord as commanded in Leviticus 23:10, *When you enter the land which I am going to give to you and reap its harvest, then you shall bring in the sheaf of the first fruits of your harvest to the priest.* This was honoring God by giving Him the best of that harvest. *Honor the LORD from your wealth and from the first of all your produce* (Proverbs 3:9). So the 144,000 were the firstfruits of the coming harvest.

The last characteristic of those who followed the Lamb was that no lie was found in their mouths, for they were blameless. Next to purity, the greatest mark of a Christian in that heathen culture was truthfulness. Has that changed much? Where is the truthfulness in our culture? But being blameless and having no lie means that no sin is hidden in the lives of those who follow the Lamb. The followers' lives are like an open book. They are without fault because they are covered by the blood of the Lamb. Psalm 32:2 says, *How blessed is the man to whom the Lord does not impute iniquity, and in whose spirit there is no deceit!* These sealed 144,000 *will do no wrong and tell no lies, nor will a deceitful tongue be found in their mouths* (Zephaniah 3:13).

When Jesus saw Nathaniel for the first time, He said, *Behold, an Israelite indeed, in whom there is no deceit!* (John 1:47). Christ meant that Nathaniel's character contained no fault, deceit, or lie. He was straightforward and honest. He was simply who he presented himself to be.

Following the Lamb in Revelation 14:1-5 means being sealed with His mark and the mark of His Father on the forehead. It means learning the song that only the redeemed can sing. Following the Lamb translates into being pure virgins for Christ and the firstfruits for God. It includes having no deceit and being utterly blameless. In other words, we are to let go of everything and try to live and act just as Jesus did when He lived here on earth.

Following the Lamb is trying to exactly imitate His actions. Is there a better definition of Christianity? If we do this, we will be sealed with His mark and able to sing a new song. We will be pure, give Him the best of our fruits and be totally honest. What a simple but powerful theme for our lives. Follow the Lamb.

DAY TWO

Fallen, Fallen

Read Revelation 14:6-8.

1. Six angels appear in Revelation 14. The first three are announcing judgments. What kind of gospel was this angel to preach?

2. Record Matthew 24:14.

3. What was the message of the first angel?

4. What was the message of the second angel?

5. Was this second message foretold? Summarize Isaiah 21:9.

6. Will this message be fulfilled? Summarize Revelation 18:2.

7. From previous lessons, what does Babylon represent in Scripture?

8. What does it mean that Babylon *has made all the nations drink of the wine of the passion of her immorality* (verse 8)?

   Jeremiah 51:7-8

   Revelation 18:3-7

The everlasting or eternal gospel preached by the first angel is to fear God and give Him the glory. Now is the time to worship the Creator. The result of not obeying the message of the first angel is to receive the consequence of the second angel's message. The second angel cries, *Fallen, fallen is Babylon the great.* Remember that in Scripture, Babylon historically represents Rome or spiritually represents evil. Babylon is a corrupting force to other nations. She was the leader in pulling them into arrogance, idolatry, harlotry, and immorality in general. While Babylon thinks she is on top of the world, her fall comes suddenly.

O. J. Simpson, a college Heisman Trophy winner, was the first professional running back to gain 2,000 yards in a career, a record that stood until 1984. To this day, only four football players have ever accomplished this. ESPN, a sports network, has listed him as the 49th best athlete of the 20th century. O. J. Simpson presented himself as gentle and well-spoken, gaining advertising endorsements and a spot on Monday Night Football as a color commentator. He was a favorite among colleagues as well as the public.

But then the shocking news came on June 17, 1994, that O. J. was fleeing from arrest by the police in his Ford Bronco. America watched in stunned silence as news shows first reported Simpson being charged with the murder of his estranged wife, Nicole Simpson, and an acquaintance, Ronald Goldman, and then his supposed getaway attempt after leaving a "suicide note." As days went by and evidence poured in, it appeared that the O. J. the public had admired was not the true man.

While Mr. Simpson was acquitted at his criminal trial, there was a great outcry in this country that justice had not been served. Later, a huge legal judgment was served against O. J., finding him liable in the wrongful death of these same two people. Was he really guilty or innocent? We may never know for sure, but we do know that, overnight, O. J. Simpson was a fallen man.

At that point, personal friends and the public in general no longer believed in him or trusted him. Everyone seemed to question whether or not he was really a killer. If so, he certainly wasn't the well-mannered hero the country had thought he was. He was possibly a criminal. While his resources were totally drained in fighting his legal battles and trying to pay off the judgment against him, he had no more means to make big money. Advertisers no longer wanted his endorsements. No sports shows wanted him on their team. No one wanted to hire him. The mighty one had fallen.

O. J. Simpson will most likely never regain the public's admiration. No matter what image he presents or what new athletic records he could achieve, that position of respect is gone forever. While evil was hidden for a time and deceit reigned, consequence and punishment now exist. That is the deceit of evil. Evil convinces its victims that they are in control. In truth, we only have power if God allows it.

Just as O. J. Simpson's fall was sudden and complete, Babylon the great and the evil she represents will be no different. It is easy for her to laugh in the face of God now as He allows her evil to reign. But while she believes she is invincible, when God chooses, her day will be over. She will fall suddenly and completely with no hope of recovery. Presently, repentance is still possible, but in that day the fall will be final. *Fallen, fallen is Babylon.*

MEMORY CHALLENGE

Write out this week's memory verse.

DAY THREE

Forehead's Mark

Read Revelation 14:9-11.

1. What will happen to the ones who receive the mark of the beast on their foreheads or hands?

2. Why will many be pressured into receiving the mark? See Revelation 13:16-17.

3. What will happen in the end to those who refuse to be pressured into receiving the mark? See Revelation 20:4.

4. In the Old Testament there were times when God protected His people with a mark. Summarize the following Scriptures.

   Exodus 12:7, 12-13

   Ezekiel 9:4-6

5. Can lives be marked by sin? Answer by summarizing the following verses.

   Isaiah 3:9

   The Living Bible says it this way: *The very look on their faces gives them away and shows their guilt.*

   Jeremiah 2:22

6. If our sin is covered by the blood of the Lamb, as in the Passover, can we be marked for God? Record the following Scriptures.

Psalm 37:37

Galatians 6:17

Daniel 3 tells Nebuchadnezzar's story of setting up the first image proclaimed by the government to be worshiped. It was a statue of gold, 90 feet tall and 9 feet wide, set up on the plain of Dura. When the command was given, all the people were to fall down and worship. *Whoever does not fall down and worship shall immediately be cast into the midst of a furnace of blazing fire* (Daniel 3:6). Three young men from the entire population of Babylon were brave enough to say they would not bow down and worship the image, for their law demanded, *You shall have no other gods before Me* (Exodus 20:3). These three—Shadrach, Meshach, and Abednego—were brought before the king and questioned as to their actions. When he was told that they would not bow down, Nebuchadnezzar asked who could deliver them out of his hands. They responded, *Our God whom we serve is able to deliver us from the furnace of blazing fire; and He will deliver us out of your hand, O king. But even if He does not, let it be known to you, O king, that we are not going to serve your gods or worship the golden image that you have set up* (Daniel 3:17-18).

The test will come back around in the Book of Revelation. All the world will be pressured into receiving the mark of the beast, which relates to worshiping the beast. The government will again promise *as many as do not worship the image of the beast to be killed* (Revelation 13:15). But just as Shadrach, Meshach, and Abednego were delivered from the fiery furnace in Daniel 3, God's people who refuse to worship the beast will be delivered in the end. Some may die in martyrdom, but reread Revelation 20:4 from today's lesson to be reminded of the final outcome. The government will try to persuade the people they will die without the mark of the beast, but the truth is they will die if they take the mark of the beast.

The beast's mark will be tangible, but each of us has an intangible mark. Our lives show the mark of our character. Are we loving, forgiving, kind, and wise? What does that tell others about our lives? Do we radiate selfishness, greed, jealousy, or judgment? That, too, tells a story. Whether we want to accept it or not, we all have a mark.

The closer we grow to Christ, the more we are "marked" by Him. Others see integrity in our character and the fruit of the Spirit in our lives.

MEMORY CHALLENGE

Read this week's memory verse aloud several times.

DAY FOUR

Faith and Deeds

Read Revelation 14:12-13.

1. According to today's Scripture, perseverance refers to keeping what two things?

2. What do you think *for their deeds follow with them* means?

3. The *Guideposts Family Concordance* defines "faith" as "confidence in the testimony of another."[1] Record the definition from Hebrews 11:1.

4. As Christians, faith is important in our lives. Summarize the following Scriptures:

   Romans 1:17

   Ephesians 2:8

   Ephesians 6:16

5. Should our deeds reflect our faith? Summarize:

   Habakkuk 2:4

   Acts 14:9-10

1 Timothy 6:11-14

6. Answer the following questions from Hebrews 11:

By faith, *men of old gained* _____ (verse 2).

What did Noah do by faith (verse 7)?

What did Moses do by faith (verse 29)?

Record verse 6.

Yesterday we learned that many would receive the mark of the beast as encouraged by the worldly government. But God has warned us not to receive the mark, for it will lead to death. In verses 12-13, Revelation 14 speaks of having the faith to obey God's commands and keep our faith in Jesus. Our deeds will reflect this faith, and then we are promised a rest from our labors.

Our faith and deeds cannot be separated. If we have faith, it will show in how we live our lives. If we do not act out our faith, one would have to question if we really have it. Our faith will really begin to show in our actions when the world tries to convince us that its ways are true. But *the conviction of things not seen*, the confidence of the testimony of Jesus is that God will ultimately win the battle for control of earth and humankind. If we want to be on the winning side, we'd better stick with Him!

All the great people in Hebrews 11 acted on their faith. Noah built an ark when there was no body of water in sight. Abraham trusted God with the sacrifice of Isaac, and Rahab hid the spies. Their faith and deeds went together. One reflected the other. They are not two separate entities but two parts of a whole. *Deeds will follow them* means that we will be rewarded for faithfulness, endurance, patience, and acts.

During times of persecution, Christians are often asked to show their faith by the deed of death in order not to rebuke the faith. During the times of tribulation this is certainly a possibility. But today we show our faith by how we live. Our deeds reflect our faith. For example, those who claim to have faith but live in criticism of fellow Christians show they really believe the Holy Spirit doesn't speak to us personally to make us more Christlike. If they believed this, their actions would be prayer to the Father and faith in the Spirit's work in fellow believers' lives. Likewise, if they say they have faith and in the midst of difficult circumstances remain peaceful, their faith is reflected in their deeds.

In his commentary on Revelation, William Barclay states, "But his [the Christian's] function now is not usually to protect the faith by being ready to die for it, but to commend it by being diligent to live for it."[2] We cannot escape our own deeds. May we be faithful in our deeds reflecting Christ.

MEMORY CHALLENGE

Who knows our frame?

DAY FIVE

Final Harvest

Read Revelation 14:14-16.

1. What was the one like who sat on the white cloud?

2. Why was the one sitting on the cloud told to put in his sickle and reap?

3. To help understand the final harvest, read the parable of the wheat and tares in Matthew 13:24-30 and 36-43. Summarize this parable.

4. Summarize the following Scriptures that portray harvesting as judgment.

   Jeremiah 51:33

   Joel 3:13

   Mark 4:29

5. What is being harvested in this final harvest? Answer by looking up the following Scriptures:

   Luke 10:1-2

   John 4:35-38

6. If the final harvest occurred today, would you be ready? If yes, praise the Lord! If no, pray and make right with God whatever stands in your way.

Revelation 14:14-16 has two characters in its drama. The first, the one like a son of man with the golden crown and sharp sickle, is believed by most commentators to be Christ. He is described in similar terms in Daniel 7:13-14 and Revelation 1:13. The angel who tells Him to harvest comes from the very presence of God for he comes from *out of the temple*. Therefore, God is giving the command.

This chapter has emphasized the faith of the Christian and being "marked" by Christ as one of His. We are told to follow the Lamb wherever He goes. Now the scene turns to judgment. We were warned against receiving the mark of the beast and now are told of the consequence. When Christ spoke of the harvest, it always involved souls. The final harvest is the final judgment of men's souls.

The verses studied today and those left for tomorrow represent two harvests, the wheat and the grapes. At this point, the symbolism becomes rather confusing, and there are many possibilities. These are clearly two different groups judged separately. The unclear part is who the two groups represent.

One possibility is that the first group is made up of Jews while the second is the Gentiles. It seems likely that the Jews covered by the blood of Christ have already been taken out of the mix as the firstfruits referred to in verse 4. It is possible that the Jews left are the ones who represent the evil Babylon. The second (grape) harvesting will be the judgment of the nation of Israel itself. Possibly Hosea 6:11 relates to this when it says, *Also, O Judah, there is a harvest appointed for you, when I restore the fortunes of My people.* Another possibility is that the righteous are harvested first and the wicked second.

Remember that some of God's words remain mysterious, and we will not understand all the details of the symbolism. What we do need to know is that there is a harvest of souls. No one escapes this judgment. Christ urged us to be workers for Him in the harvest. He wants us to represent Him to the world and bring Him a full harvest of children. May we strive to be found in the righteous harvest, having brought with us many brothers and sisters.

MEMORY CHALLENGE

Fill in the blanks:

For He Himself _____ our _____; He is _____ that we are but _____.

Psalm 103:14

Fully Ripe

Read Revelation 14:17-20.

1. Briefly summarize today's scripture.

2. Read the parable of the vineyard in Isaiah 5:1-7 and summarize it.

3. Summarize what Jesus said about the vine and the branches in John 15:1-6.

4. Who is the vine in the Isaiah passage and in the John passage? Who are the vinedresser and branches?

5. He who abides in Christ is to bear _____ (John 15:5).

6. What are the fruit of the Spirit? See Galatians 5:22-23.

Throughout the Old Testament, Israel was the vineyard of God. These were His chosen people and as the Great Vinedresser this was His own vineyard. When Christ came it was to include all humankind in God's vineyard. He came to save all that would call upon His name as Lord and receive the forgiveness of sins from Him. Christ himself would become the Vine, and we, His people, the branches in God's vineyard. Without the Vine we would be nothing. But with the Vine, we would be a cherished part of the Vine that would produce fruit. The fruit would be the fruit of the Spirit—love, joy, peace, patience, kindness, goodness, faithfulness, gentleness, and self-control.

Just as with the wheat and tares, some of this fruit in the vineyard would not be good. If our fruit is not the fruit of the Spirit, it is the fruit of lawlessness. *Now the deeds of the flesh are evident, which are: immorality, impurity, sensuality, idolatry, sorcery, enmities, strife, jealousy, outbursts of anger, disputes, dissensions, factions, envying, drunkenness, carousing, and things like these* (Galatians 5:19-21). Our lives produce good or bad fruit, and we will be judged accordingly. If the *firstfruits* or fruit of the Spirit is gone, this harvesting of grapes yields fruit that is useless.

During harvest, grapes are thrown into a winepress that has two troughs. The upper trough is the one where the workers can stand and squash the grapes with their feet. Then there is a gutterlike trough through which the wine flows into the tub or trough to be bottled. In this judgment picture, the fully ripe grapes are pressed and the wine becomes blood. It flows so freely that it is as high as a horse's bridle (or four feet high) and flows 200 miles. This is the length of Palestine from north to south. Possibly this represents judgment that covers all of Israel and is a total blotting out of evil. *Fully ripe* may be an understatement.

The 14th chapter of Revelation goes back and forth between the goodness of God's people and their reward and the judgment of the evil. Today's lesson concerning harvesting these grapes that are fully ripe is no different. Let's not get lost in the sadness of the judgment, but focus on the goodness of the reward. We can also experience a little bit of God's blessing and beauty here on earth by demonstrating the fruit of the spirit (love, joy, peace, patience, goodness, kindness, faithfulness, gentleness, and self-control) to each other. Blessed be His name!

Written by Linda Shaw

Write out this week's verse from memory.

Revelation

■ **A Study of Revelation 15**

DAY ONE

Comparisons

Read Revelation 15:1-8.

1. What great sign did John see in heaven?

The pouring out of the seven bowls of the wrath of God is the third of a series of sevens that has formed the structure of the Book of Revelation. The conviction that judgments must fall before the coming of the kingdom of God begins in the teachings of the Old Testament prophets concerning the day of the Lord (typical references—Amos 5:18 ff., Isaiah 2:12 ff.). No passage in the New Testament is more closely related to this prediction than the words of Jesus recorded in Mark 13, Matthew 24, and Luke 21 when Jesus teaches His disciples on the Mount of Olives, just east of Jerusalem.

2. Comparing Jesus' words of warning and John's words of judgment concerning the seven seals, how are each of these passages similar?

Jesus	*Seals*
Example:	
Mark 13:7 wars and rumors of war	Revelation 6:2— a cold war by the Antichrist
Mark 13:8*a*	Revelation 6:4
Mark 13:8*b*	Revelation 6:12
Mark 13:24	Revelation 6:12
Luke 21:11	Revelation 6:8*b*
Luke 21:12	Revelation 6:9

The bowl judgments bear a striking similarity to the plagues of the exodus.

The 10 plagues were aimed at the gods of Egypt and were designed to give proof of the power of the God of Israel over the gods of Egypt. Over and over in Exodus it is re-peated that by these miracles both Israelites and Egyptians would come to know that the Lord is God (6:7; 7:5, 17; 8:22; 10:2; 14:4, 18). The ten plagues were: waters of the Nile turned to blood, frogs, lice, flies, disease on cattle, boils, hail, locusts, darkness, and death of their firstborn.

The sufferings of the Israelites under their taskmasters foreshadow the more terrible persecution of the Christians at the hands of the Antichrist's agents. However, the judgments of the Lord on the land of Egypt pale in comparison to the greater judgments that are to fall on the kingdom of the beast. The deliverance from Egypt is far surpassed by the redemption of the Lamb, as the saints rejoice in their resurrection.

Beasley-Murray in *The New Century Bible Commentary* defines these parallels between the judgments of the seven trumpets and the seven bowls:

Trumpets

1. Hail, fire, and blood fall on the earth, one-third of which is burned up.

2. A blazing mountain falls into the sea. One-third of the sea becomes blood, a third of the sea creatures die, and a third of ships are destroyed.

3. A blazing star (Wormwood) falls on one-third of rivers and fountains; their waters are poisoned and many die.

4. One-third of sun, moon, and stars are struck. Darkness results for one-third of a night and day.

5. The shaft of the pit is opened. Sun and air are darkened with smoke from which locusts emerge to torment men without the seal of God.

6. Four angels bound at the Euphrates are released, with their 200 million cavalry. One-third of the men are killed by them.

7. Loud voices in heaven announce the coming of the kingdom of God and of Christ. Lightning, thunder, earthquake, and hail occur.

Bowls

1. A bowl is poured on the earth. Malignant sores come on men who had the mark of the beast and worshiped his image.

2. A bowl is poured on the seas. The sea becomes blood, and every living thing in it dies.

3. A bowl is poured on rivers and fountains, and they become blood.

4. A bowl is poured on the sun, which scorches men with fire.

5. A bowl is poured on the throne of the beast. His kingdom is darkened and men are in anguish.

6. A bowl is poured on the Euphrates, which dries up for kings from the East. Kings of the world assemble for battle at Armageddon.

7. A bowl is poured into the air, a loud voice from God's throne announces, "It is done." Lightning, thunder, and an unprecedented earthquake occur, and terrible hail falls.[1]

3. Why did John refer to the plagues he saw as the *seven last plagues?*

We have gone through the whole range of God's judgments. This time there is a declaration of finality. These are the last plagues. Judgment is complete. This does not mean there is no relevance for us today. While these judgments refer especially to the end times, we remember that throughout the Bible, those who obey His Word are blessed, and the disobedient suffer judgment.

Martyrs Win

Read Revelation 15:2.

1. How did John describe the part of heaven revealed to him?

2. Looking back to Revelation 4:6, how was the sea of glass described?

3. Who did John see standing before him?

4. What are the martyrs holding?

5. Can the beast, his image, and his number be conquered?

6. What has God provided that we can use today in our battle to be victorious over Satan?

John has used the Old Testament to teach us about God's judgment and grace. The seven angels have bowls of wrath (plagues) to pour on a wicked world. They remind us of the plagues God sent to Egypt in the days of Moses (Exodus 7—12). God delivered Israel from Egypt, and they sang a song of victory at the Red Sea (Exodus 15). John saw the victors of the Tribulation singing by the heavenly sea of glass. This is the same sea of glass before the throne of God described in Revelation 4:6. However, an extraordinary change can be seen. The sea is mingled with fire, causing it to be fiery red in color. This is a passage of judgment, and fire in the Scripture is often the symbol of judgment.

7. Record these verses:

Exodus 9:24

Matthew 3:12 (the last phrase)

Hebrews 12:29

In the Old Testament, the Israelites were able to pass through the Red Sea to escape Pharaoh and his oppression. In Revelation we read that the Christian martyrs, those who had conquered the beast—who had refused to worship his image or have the number of his name on their foreheads—have made their escape across the heavenly Red Sea from their persecutor. They stand before the throne holding harps of God.

In *The Daily Study Bible*, William Barclay enlarges our understanding of martyrdom. "It is said that the martyrs have emerged victorious and conquerors from their contest with the forces of Antichrist. There is something very significant here. The martyrs died, and they died the most savage and cruel and agonizing deaths and yet they are said to have emerged victorious. It was the very fact that they had died that made them victors. If they had remained alive by being false to their faith, they would have been defeated. Again and again the records of the Early Church describe a day of martyrdom as a day of victory. In the record of the martyrdom of Saint Perpetua we read: "'The day of their victory dawned, and they walked from prison to the amphitheater as if they were walking to heaven, happy and serene in countenance.' It can often happen that death is a greater victory than survival, and that survival is defeat. Jesus said, *For whoever wishes to save his life will lose it; but whoever loses his life for My sake will find it* (Matthew 16:25). The real victory is not to live in safety, to evade trouble, cautiously and prudently to preserve life; the real victory is to face the worst that evil can do, and if need be, to be faithful unto death."[1]

In Lesson 12, Day 5, a reference was given of a present-day martyr, Cassie Bernall, who was killed April 20, 1999, in the massacre at Columbine High School in Littleton, Colorado. On May 25, 1999, Dr. Ed Tropp, associate pastor of Circle Drive Baptist Church in Colorado Springs, stated: "The news media is not reporting what they don't understand, a revival has begun. Christian kids in public schools in the whole area that had been embarrassed because they wanted to be cool and didn't want to stand up for Christ, have boldly spoken of their commitment to Christ, and now hundreds of teenagers have turned to Jesus Christ. One girl answered, 'Yes, I believe in Jesus,' and what that has done in the hearts of the people in this community is unbelievable."

Lord, give me the courage of a 17-year-old, not just to die for Jesus, but to live for Jesus.

8. Describe your reactions to these insights into martyrdom.

MEMORY CHALLENGE

How are the days of man described?

DAY THREE

Martyrs Sing

Read Revelation 15:3-4.

1. What are the saints in heaven doing?

2. What attributes of God are praised in their singing?

3. List the names of God used in the song.

4. What is your favorite hymn or worship song? Why?

5. What is one practical step you can take to include singing in your worship of God?

In our study of Revelation 6 in verses 9-11, the martyrs were under the altar in heaven crying out for vengeance upon their persecutors. They were told to rest until their number was completed. In today's study the number of martyrs is complete; all have crossed the symbolic Red Sea to a place of safety in heaven, and their enemies are near to being judged by God. Consequently, instead of praying for divine vengeance as before, they now sing a song of praise to God for their liberation. It is called *the song of Moses, the bond-servant of God*, in remembering the song sung by Moses and the children of Israel following the miraculous passage through the Red Sea (Exodus 15:1). It is also called *the song of the Lamb*, for it was through Him that they have been saved.

6. The song of the martyrs is almost entirely composed of Scripture from the Old Testament. Record phrases that correspond to words of their song:

   Great and marvelous are Your works.
       Example: Psalm 92:5: *How great are Thy works, O Lord!*

Righteous and true are Your ways.
   Psalm 145:17

Who will not fear, O Lord, and glorify Your name?
   Psalm 86:9

For You alone are holy.
   1 Samuel 2:2

ALL THE NATIONS WILL COME AND WORSHIP BEFORE YOU.
   Psalm 86:9

YOUR RIGHTEOUS ACTS HAVE BEEN REVEALED.
   Psalm 98:2

When the martyrs wanted words to praise God for His goodness and His greatness, it was in the Scriptures they found them.

In the song of the victorious martyrs, there is no mention of their own achievement and victory. The whole song praises the greatness of God. Heaven is a place where men forget their own triumphs and remember only God. Heaven is heaven because self-importance is lost in the presence of the greatness and the glory of God.

The scriptural song of the martyrs serves as a model for us. The Memory Challenge for our study of the Book of Revelation is Psalm 103. As you read it, personalized, from *The Living Bible*, let it be a song from your innermost heart to your loving Father God who longs to hear your songs of worshipful praise.

   I bless Your holy name, God, with all of my heart. Yes, I bless You, Lord, and I have not forgotten the glorious things You do for me. You forgive my sins. You heal me. You ransom me from hell. You surround me with lovingkindness and tender mercies. You fill my life with good things. My youth is renewed like the eagle's. You give justice to me when I am treated unfairly. You revealed Your will and nature to Moses and the people of Israel.

   You are merciful and tender to me when I don't deserve it; You are slow to anger and full of kindness and love. You never bear a grudge toward me nor remain angry with me. You have not punished me as I deserve for all my sins, for Your mercy toward me who fears and honors You is as great as the heights of the heavens above the earth. You have removed my sins as far away from me as the east is from the west.

You are like a father to me, tender and sympathetic to me who reverences You. You know I am but dust and that my days are few and brief, like grass, like flowers, blown by the wind and gone forever.

Your lovingkindness is from everlasting to everlasting, to me who reverences You; Your salvation is to my children's children because I am faithful to Your covenant and remember to obey You!

You have made the heaven Your throne; from there You rule over everything there is. Bless the Lord, you mighty angels of His who carry out His orders, listening for each of His commands. Yes, bless the Lord, you armies of the angels who serve Him constantly. Let everything everywhere bless the Lord, and how I bless Him too!

MEMORY CHALLENGE

Fill in the blanks:

As for man, his days are like _____; as a

_____ of the field, so he _____.

Psalm 103:15

DAY FOUR

The Temple Is Opened

Read Revelation 15:5.

1. What did John see opened in heaven?

2. In Revelation 11:19, what was opened?

   What appeared when it was opened?

The temple refers to the inner holy place of the Tabernacle—it is also known as the holy of holies. *The tabernacle of the testimony* refers to the total Tabernacle structure that God instructed Moses to build.

3. In Exodus 25, God is speaking to Moses. Record Exodus 25:8.

The Tabernacle of God in the wilderness of Sinai is the first habitation that the living God ever caused to be built for Him. During the 40 days and nights Moses spent on the holy mountain, he received not only the tablets with the commandments of God but also God's instructions for building His Tabernacle. Fifty chapters in the Bible record His instructions concerning the Tabernacle: 13 in Exodus, 18 in Leviticus, 13 in Numbers, 2 in Deuteronomy, and 4 in Hebrews.

Paul F. Kiene, author of *The Tabernacle of God in the Wilderness of Sinai*, defines the Tabernacle of God as "the place where He manifested His glory in judgment and grace, the dwelling place of the Almighty among His people on the basis of the expiatory offering."[1] An expiatory offering is given for the removal of guilt through the payment of the required penalty for their sin. These included the burnt offering (Leviticus 1:3-17), the peace offering (3:1-7), the sin offering (4:1—5:13), and the guilt offering (5:15—6:6).

God's grace is clearly shown; He did not simply wait for His people to bring before Him the appropriate sacrifices,

He took the initiative in specifying which sacrifices would be needed. The Old Testament promises assure us that God remains gracious even in our sinning, and He stands ready to forgive even before we are ready to repent.

4. Summarize Isaiah 65:2.

By the expiation (removal) of human guilt through the required sacrifices, the wrath of God is turned away, and the holiness of God is satisfied. In the New Testament it is God himself who in the person of His Son, Jesus, performs the sacrifice of expiation (becomes the sacrifice). It is God who in the person of His Son within himself swallows up evil and substitutes himself as the sacrifice for the sin of His people. A sacrifice was necessary to satisfy the demands of His law, but God himself provided the sacrifice out of His incomparable love. Hebrews 10 emphasizes the finality of Christ's sacrifice by contrasting it with the lack of finality of the Old Testament system of law and sacrifices.

5. Record Hebrews 10:3-4.

Christ's redemption does not need to be repeated. Therefore, a rejection of His sacrifice is final and unforgivable (Hebrews 10:29-31). What human ritual offerings could not do, God has done by giving up His Son for the sins of the whole human race.

6. Personalize John 3:16.

7. Pray a prayer of thanksgiving for your salvation.

As John looks intently on the scene of his vision, the temple is opened, that is, the curtain (veil) is parted, and seven angels are seen coming out of the temple. The temple (the holy place) into which the high priest alone could go, and only after proper sacrifices, does not exclude holy angels who have no sin.

MEMORY CHALLENGE

Review Psalm 103:15 until you can quote the verse by memory.

DAY FIVE

Seven Angels

Read Revelation 15:6-7.

1. Who came out of the temple?

2. How did John describe them?

3. Who do these scriptures identify as wearing white clothing?

    Matthew 17:2

    Revelation 3:5

    Revelation 4:4

    Revelation 19:7-8

4. What was given to the seven angels and by whom?

5. Looking back to Revelation 4:7, describe the four creatures.

In *The Daily Study Bible*, William Barclay explains Revelation 15:6-7:

> The seven angels come out from the place where the Law of God rests (the ten commandments in the ark of the covenant). They are coming out to demonstrate the righteous Law of God; they are coming out to show by their avenging action that no man and no nation can with impunity (an exemption from punishment) defy the Law of God. The procession of the angels from the tabernacle symbolically shows that they are coming out from the resting place of the Divine Law to vindicate that, and to show that it cannot be disobeyed.
>
> They are clothed in a shining white robe, and they are girded about the breasts with a golden girdle. The

robes of the angels are symbolic of three things. (1) Their dress is a priestly dress. The robe of white fine linen and the gold embroidered girdle about the breast is the dress of the High Priest. The High Priest might well be called God's representative among men; and these angels come forth as the avenging representatives of God. (2) Their dress is royal dress. The white linen and the high girdle is the garment of princes and of kings. And these angels come forth with the royalty of the King of kings upon them. (3) The gleaming white robe is the dress of one from heaven. The young man at the empty tomb of Christ was clothed in a long white garment (Mark 16:5; Matthew 28:3). The angels are the inhabitants of heaven, come to execute God's decrees upon earth.[1]

Their clothing shows that they are free from corruption, immorality, and injustice. They are righteous in action. They come out of the inner sanctuary of the temple. They leave His presence to face a world that has reached the height of wickedness.

As the four living creatures called forth the four horsemen at the opening of the seal judgments (Revelation 6), so it is one of these supreme representatives of the holy God who gives *the seven angels seven golden bowls full of the wrath of God*. In the righteous government of God, those nations that have oppressed and sought the destruction of His people must be given the fierceness of His wrath. His righteousness demands the punishment of iniquity, both in this world and in that which is to come.

MEMORY CHALLENGE

Fill in the blank review:

Bless the LORD, O my _____, and all that is within me, _____ His holy _____. Bless the LORD, O my soul, and _____ none of His _____, who _____ all your iniquities, who _____ all your diseases; who _____ your life from the _____, who _____ you with lovingkindness and _____; who _____ your years with _____ _____, so that your _____ is renewed like the _____. The LORD performs _____ deeds and _____ for all who are _____. He made known His ways to _____, His acts to the sons of _____.

Psalm 103:1-7

Dwelling Places of God

Read Revelation 15:8.

1. What events took place in the heavenly temple after the angels were dispatched with their plagues?

Consider how this scene relates to the completion of the Tabernacle in Exodus 40.

Exodus 40:33-38: *Moses finished the work* [on the Tabernacle]. *Then the cloud covered the tent of meeting, and the glory of the LORD filled the Tabernacle. Moses was not able to enter the tent of meeting because the cloud had settled on it, and the glory of the LORD filled the tabernacle. Throughout all their journeys whenever the cloud was taken up from over the tabernacle, the sons of Israel would set out; but if the cloud was not taken up, then they did not set out until the day when it was taken up. For throughout all their journeys, the cloud of the LORD was on the tabernacle by day, and there was fire in it by night, in the sight of all the houses of Israel.*

Two things made the Tabernacle a special structure:

(1) The pattern was given by God.

(2) God's glorious presence filled it when He came to dwell with His people.

What a gracious God who chose to dwell with such a rebellious people!

Solomon's Temple was a place of glory (1 Kings 8:1-12). However, despite its extraordinary beauty, it was just another building until God moved in and consecrated it.

2. Read 1 Kings 8:10-13. Record verses 11-12.

Exodus 19:17-18, 21 (at the time God gave the law to Moses at Sinai): *And Moses brought the people out of the camp to meet God, and they stood at the foot of the mountain. Now Mount Sinai was all in smoke because the LORD descended upon it in fire; and its smoke ascended like the smoke of a furnace, and the whole mountain quaked violently. . . . Then the LORD spoke to Moses,*

"Go down, warn the people, so that they do not break through to the LORD to gaze, and many of them perish."

The smoke is the evidence of *the glory of God and . . . His power* (Revelation 15:8), and its manifestation signifies the presence of the glorious and powerful God himself. It is the awesome holiness of that Presence that forbids any to come near *so that they do not . . . perish* (Exodus 19:21).

3. Warren W. Wiersbe, in his *Chapter-By-Chapter Bible Commentary*, has made an interesting progression of God's dwelling places:

   (1) First, God walked with man . . . (name two)

   _____ (Genesis 5:24)

   _____ (Genesis 6:9)

   . . . then He desired to _____ with him (Exodus 25:8).

   (2) His glory came into the _____ (Exodus 40:34), . . . but when Israel sinned, the glory _____ (1 Samuel 4:21-22).

   (3) The glory dwelt in the _____ (1 Kings 8:10-11), . . . but then departed again because of the sins of the people (Ezekiel 11:21-23).

   (4) The glory came in the person of _____ _____ (John 1:14, 17), . . . and now dwells in _____ individually (1 Corinthians 6:19-20) and the Church collectively (Ephesians 2:20-22).

   (5) One day God's glory will be revealed in a new heaven and earth and a perfect city where His people will dwell _____ (Revelation 21-22).[1]

4. Read Hebrews 10:19-22. Summarize 10:19-20.

The same Savior who died for you now lives for you and invites you to come into His presence (the holy place) to worship and share your needs. The Old Testament high priest could go behind the veil only once a year, but we can come into God's presence anytime.

Be sure you are cleansed and prepared to meet Him. You can trust Him who promised to be faithful (Hebrews 10:23).

Revelation 15:8 suggests that not even an angel can approach the Lord's presence to intercede for earth now that judgments are about to fall. God himself is present in His majesty and glory to perform His judgments and establish His kingdom in power. The angels with the bowl-like cups are instruments in the hands of God, the almighty Judge. They empty the cups. He acts.

Think of those you know who are unbelievers. Enter into His holy place and tell God about them and ask Him to convict their hearts. Let Him speak to you concerning further responsibility you may have for them. As judgment nears, God's heart breaks for sinners who ignore His call for repentance.

Guide us, Father.

Written by Marie Coody

MEMORY CHALLENGE

Fill in the blanks review:

The LORD is _____ and _____, slow to _____ and abounding in _____. He will not always _____ with us; nor will He keep His _____ forever. He has not _____ with us according to our _____, nor _____ us according to our _____. For as high as the _____ are above the earth, so great is His _____ toward those who _____ Him. As far as the _____ is from the _____, so far has He removed our _____ from us. Just as a _____ has compassion on his _____, so the LORD has _____ on those who _____ Him. For He Himself knows our _____; He is mindful that we are but _____. As for man, his _____ are like _____; as a _____ of the field, so he _____.

Psalm 103:8-15

Revelation

LESSON 16

■ A Study of Revelation 16

DAY ONE

Words

Read Revelation 16. Review verses 1-2.

1. What did John hear from the heavenly temple?

2. What words were given to the seven angels?

3. Who was speaking this word from the temple? (Refer to 15:8.)

4. What happened when the first angel emptied his bowl?

5. How is this a partial fulfillment of the warning to the angel in 14:9-10?

6. Summarize Exodus 9:8-11.

7. How is the first plague appropriate for those who have allowed *the mark of the beast* on their bodies?

8. Suppose *the mark of the beast* represents compromise and accommodation to culture. Find and record a scripture that gives confidence and courage to be an overcomer under extreme pressure of the enemy.

From the beginning of God's Word to the end, there is a continuity in the punishment of evil. From the cloud on Mount Sinai, God gave Moses many instructions and warnings regarding blessings for obedience and curses (punishment) for disobedience.

Revelation chapters 2 and 3 show the patience of God as He warns the churches of their sins. To each church He gives an opportunity for repentance. He closes each letter to the churches with, *He who has an ear, let him hear what the Spirit says to the churches*, and He follows with a promise of heaven to those who obey (overcome).

9. Summarize the following verses:

   Malachi 2:2

   1 John 5:5

MEMORY CHALLENGE

Psalm 103:16

When the wind has passed over it, it is no more, and its place acknowledges it no longer.

The unique concept of a spoken word is important for understanding the significance of both blessing and cursing. According to Old Testament thought patterns, the spoken word had the power of its own fulfillment. When Isaac mistakenly blessed Jacob rather than Esau, he could not take back the blessing, for the words of the blessing had been spoken (Genesis 27:18-41). Isaac knew his blessing was permanently given to Jacob. His spoken word had its own fulfillment and now existed in history.

Can a spoken word have the power of its own fulfillment in a life today? What keeps people from turning to God? Can it be the fulfillment of the words they have spoken?

Words. What words find their fulfillment in your heart? Words are like seeds. We must be aware of the words we allow to germinate in our hearts. We must recognize the evil words (seeds) and remove them while we nourish the good words and let them come to their fulfillment in our lives. Does your heart receive, then obey God's Word? God's Word is good seed. It has life and power to produce a harvest of blessing in your life.

A wonderful example of a harvest of blessing is the life of Joseph (Genesis 37—50). Joseph, at the age of 17, was not the humble, godly Joseph of chapter 45 when he so lovingly revealed his identity to his brothers. At 17, Joseph was a tattletale, bringing Jacob bad reports of his brothers. He flaunted his coat of many colors, reflecting Jacob's partiality to him, causing his brothers to hate him. Joseph abused the gift God had given him by not keeping the revelation of the dreams to himself. Joseph was not ready to be used of God. His attitude and the words he spoke displayed not only his self-centeredness but also his self-righteousness (37:2-11).

The jealous brothers cast Joseph into an empty pit with no water or food (37:24). While he was in the pit, what do you believe Joseph was thinking? Scripture doesn't tell, but his dreams were shattered and he had no reason to hope that he would be rescued. He was in an impossible situation and, humanly speaking, his life could be over. Don't you believe that he prayed to God?

His brothers took him from the pit and sold him to Ishmaelite traders. *The LORD was with Joseph* (39:2). This time in Joseph's life seems to be the beginning of a dramatic change; from the self-righteous son of Jacob, he became the godly, obedient slave of Potiphar, a member of the personal staff of Pharaoh, king of Egypt. He became a trustworthy servant of Potiphar and an obedient son of God (verses 1-5).

Joseph fled temptation with the words, *How then could I do this great evil and sin against God?* (verse 9). He endured unjust punishment in prison, then again became a favored worker with supervision of the prison. When he was 30 years old, he became a ruler over Egypt, second only to Pharaoh.

Genesis 45 records the great reconciliation of Joseph and his brothers and soon his father, Jacob, and all of Jacob's children and their families moved to Egypt.

Joseph could have become a very bitter man. He had endured many injustices. When his brothers came to Egypt for grain, he could have refused them. He had the power to treat them in any way he chose. But Joseph changed from a self-righteous, thoughtless son and brother to a God-centered man who totally forgave the injustices that had hurt him. He refused to let words of bitterness grow in his heart. He filled his thoughts with obeying God and taking a stand for Him when called upon to do so.

Those being judged in Revelation 16 have received warnings of the last days, but they will not repent. Words of deceit and evil have taken root in their hearts, and they can no longer accept Truth.

Think, for a moment, of your unsaved loved ones. Sinners such as they are allowing wrong words to grow in their hearts. Seeds planted in fertile soil and watered from time to time do not remain seeds. They grow. Evil words in hearts don't just rest there. They grow and grow. Hearts become harder and harder. Warnings of judgment don't rouse a desire to change in the hearts of sinners. Like Pharaoh, they refuse to change and often become full of pride in their deceived hearts, believing that they do not need God.

In Matthew 13:24-30, Jesus tells the parable of the wheat and tares (weeds). At the end of the age, He will separate the true from the false and the good from the bad. Today we are growing—becoming mature wheat or full-grown weeds. He who has spiritual ears, *let him hear.*

DAY TWO

Righteous Judge

Read Revelation 16:3-7.

1. What happened when the second angel emptied his bowl into the sea?

2. What were the results of the third angel pouring out his bowl into the rivers and springs?

3. What was the responsibility of the angels in the following verses?

   Revelation 7:1

   Revelation 14:18

   Revelation 16:5

4. How did the angel of the waters describe God?

5. Did the angel of the waters approve of God's judgments that had been poured into the waters of the earth?

6. Why were the judgments that John witnessed called just?

7. How did the altar describe God's judgments?

8. Read Daniel 9:14. How did Daniel describe God when he prayed for Israel in their disobedience?

Water is necessary for life. The Bible states that God made water a part of His creation and that He exercises sovereignty over it (Isaiah 40:12). He controls the natural processes of precipitation and evaporation, as well as the courses of bodies of water (Psalm 33:7; 107:33; Proverbs 8:29). God normally assures the provision of water for human needs (Deuteronomy 11:14). However, water is sometimes used in punishment for sin, as with the flood in Noah's day (Genesis 6:17) or the drought proclaimed by Elijah (1 Kings 17:1). The divine control of water teaches people obedience to and dependency on God.

The second bowl plague, like that of the second trumpet (Revelation 8:8-9), is derived from the first Egyptian plague in which the water was turned to blood, making the water foul and killing all the fish (Exodus 7:14-25). The effects of the second bowl were even more disastrous, for when it was emptied upon the sea, *it became blood like that of a dead man*, foul and coagulated, killing all life that was in it.

The woe of the third bowl turns the fresh water supply into blood. Now there is no water to drink. Rivers and springs offer men death instead of life. The men who had shed the blood of saints and prophets find that their acts of violence have not come to an end with the death of their victims. Blood they have shed, blood they must drink. *"VENGEANCE IS MINE, I WILL REPAY," says the Lord* (Romans 12:19).

The angel of water, echoing phrases of the song of Moses and of the Lamb (Revelation 15:3-4), agrees that these judgments of God are just. The judgments are just because those who are now being punished shed the blood of martyrs (saints and prophets). People must choose whether to drink the blood of saints or wear robes dipped in the blood of the Lamb!

That an altar should speak is not surprising in a book where an eagle, a dragon, beasts from the sea and land, and other nonhuman creatures are given the power of speech. The words coming from the altar represent the fulfillment of the prayer of the martyrs under the altar (6:10), beseeching God to avenge their blood on the peoples of the earth who have persecuted and slain them. Now that His judgment has arrived, the altar speaking for the martyrs affirms that it is just. The punishment fits the crime.

The Bible teaches that God is righteous:

Ezra 9:15: *O LORD God of Israel, You art righteous . . .*
Psalm 116:5: *Gracious is the LORD, and righteous . . .*
Psalm 119:142: *Your righteousness is an everlasting righteousness . . .*
Psalm 145:17: *The LORD is righteous in all His ways . . .*
Jeremiah 12:1: *Righteous are You, O LORD . . .*
John 17:25: *O righteous Father . . .*

To be just or righteous is to have the kind of character that leads us to always do that which is right. The righteousness or justice of God is that attribute that causes Him to always do right. Holiness seems to refer to God's character as He is in himself; righteousness refers to His character as manifested in His dealings with others. Psalm 11:4-7 explains how His righteousness is manifested: *The LORD is in His holy temple; the LORD's throne is in heaven; His eyes behold, His eyelids test [closely watch,* TLB*] the sons of men. The LORD tests the righteous and the wicked, and the one who loves violence His soul hates. Upon the wicked He will rain snares; fire and brimstone and burning wind will be the portion of their cup. For the LORD is righteous, He loves righteousness; the upright will behold His face.*

No matter what the unbelieving world may say, God's judgments are righteous. Sinners reap what they sow. Because *righteousness and justice are the foundation of His throne* (Psalm 97:2), nobody can accuse God of being unfair. *His righteousness endures forever* (Psalm 111:3).

MEMORY CHALLENGE

Our time on earth is brief. Write out Psalm 103:15-16.

DAY THREE

Sunburned

Read Revelation 16:8-9.

1. Describe the judgment of the fourth bowl.

2. Read 2 Peter 3. List at least three warnings given by Peter in his letter to believers.

3. Revelation 16:9 explains that the reaction of evil men to the fierce heat of the sun was to blaspheme God. They would not repent *so as to give Him glory.* Summarize 2 Corinthians 4:4, which gives us an understanding of these deceived ones.

4. Have you ever been severely burned? If so, describe the feeling of pain.

The skin is a living tissue; even brief heating above 1200°F damages its cells. First-degree burns cause reddening of the skin and affect only the epidermis (the top layer of the skin). Such burns heal quickly, but the damaged skin may peel away after a day or two. Extensive first-degree burns (such as a sunburn) cause pain, restlessness, headache, and fever, but they are not life-threatening.

Second-degree burns damage the skin more deeply, causing blisters. However, some of the dermis (deep layer of skin) is left to recover, and these burns usually heal without scarring, unless they are very extensive.

Third-degree burns destroy the full skin thickness. The affected area will look white or charred and if the burn is very deep, muscles and bones may be exposed. Even if very localized, these burns will need specialized treatment and skin grafts to prevent scarring. In second- or third-degree burns affecting more than 10 percent of the body surface, the victim will be in shock with a low blood pressure and rapid pulse. This is caused by the loss of large quantities of fluid (and its constituent proteins) from the burned area. It may be fatal if not treated by intravenous fluid replacement.

When skin is burned, it can no longer protect the body from contamination by airborne bacteria. The infection of extensive burns may cause fatal complications if effective antibiotic treatment is not given.

With the emptying of the fourth bowl on the sun, its power is greatly increased so that men are scorched with its great heat. The life-giving heat from the sun suddenly becomes humankind's enemy with its torturous heat of destruction. Those whose burning passions had been their moral undoing burn with a fire that brings increased suffering, added to the thirst caused by the third bowl.

The purpose of the increased heat of the sun is to scorch and torture the wicked, not to consume them and the world with fire. Over larger and larger areas God allows forces of nature to turn against humankind.

Apparently, even at this stage of human history, the time of God's final outpouring of wrath and judgment upon the earth, it is not too late to repent. But God is cursed instead, *and they did not repent so as to give Him glory.*

The scorching sun shines upon men who have become so evil that they have no thought of repentance. With furious hatred *they blasphemed the name of God.* The good that had died in them had made them incapable of repentance. Just as we wonder why it took 10 disastrous plagues to make Pharaoh and the Egyptians relent and permit the Israelites to leave, so we may be amazed that these series of apocalyptic woes in Revelation will have little or no effect upon the attitude and behavior of evil people.

MEMORY CHALLENGE

Fill in the blanks:

As for _____, his days are like _____;

as a _____ of the field, so he

_____. When the _____ has

passed over it, it is no more, and its _____

acknowledges it no longer.

Psalm 103:15-16

Total Darkness

Read Revelation 16:10-11.

1. What happened when the fifth angel poured out his bowl on the beast (Satan)?

2. What are some other names for Satan that you can recall?

3. Describe your reactions to being in total darkness.

David McCord gives a vivid description of darkness in his book, *The King Is Coming:*

> I remember as a child visiting the Carlsbad Caverns in New Mexico with my parents. At a certain point down in the depths of the cave the guide had us sit down on concrete benches. Then, after he had warned us, all the lights were turned off. I have never experienced such total blackness in my life. My eyes strained toward the outermost reaches of the cavern for some glimmer of gray, some form or outline, but none was there.
>
> For a moment it seemed that we were suspended in the midst of this blackness, and that if I were to fall, I might fall in any direction. I clutched the bench tightly. My heart beat faster. I felt lost, alone and afraid, although my shoulder was pressed hard against my mother's side.
>
> When the lights came back on I felt very relieved, if a bit foolish. Nothing had changed except for the light—wonderful, beautiful light! Afraid of the dark! You bet I was![1]

It is easy to understand why darkness produces anxiety and causes anguish. If there are hazards they become much more dangerous in the darkness. Enemies become more fearsome, for without sight you are left virtually defenseless. You may become lost whether you move or remain immobile. Darkness holds the power to produce fear, confusion, lostness, panic, immobility, loneliness, anxiety, and anguish. Such is the judgment of the fifth bowl.

In one of the most terrible pictures in the Book of Revelation, we see men in the dark cursing God. The sores inflicted in the first judgment were aggravated and enlarged by the burning heat of the third judgment. Nothing was left but suffering. None of the activities of life could go on. To live at all you must have oceans, rivers and springs, and sunshine; when all these have been destroyed, life becomes hopeless.

In darkness, tormented from the pain caused by the scorching sun and the sores, people gnaw their tongues in anguish but still refuse to repent of their sins. Even in these circumstances, it is possible to continue grimly with an unrepentant heart. The Scriptures plainly refute the belief that the wicked will quickly repent when faced with catastrophic warnings of judgment; when confronted with righteous judgment of God, their blasphemy is more vile and their evil is accentuated.

The fifth angel poured his bowl on the throne of the beast, and his kingdom was plunged into an unexplained darkness, symbolizing the removal of moral light—light from God. All sense of truth and righteousness, or even of God himself, is lost. It foreshadows that terrible *outer darkness* (Matthew 8:12) into which Jesus says those who are unrepentant will be cast.

MEMORY CHALLENGE

Read Psalm 103:15 and 16 together, then repeat them as one thought.

DAY FIVE

Dried Up

Read Revelation 16:12-16.

1. What happened to the Euphrates River when the sixth angel emptied his bowl into the river?

2. There are a number of times in the Old Testament when the drying up of the waters is a sign and an action of the power of God. Record the phrase from the following scriptures that tell of these times:

   Moses and the Israelites at the Red Sea (Exodus 14:21):

   Joshua and all of Israel at the Jordan River (Joshua 3:17):

   God's people at the Sea of Egypt (Isaiah 11:15):

   The threat of God's vengeance against Babylon (Jeremiah 51:36):

   God's protection of His people as they return to Israel (Zechariah 10:11):

3. In Revelation 16:13, John saw three evil spirits disguised as frogs. Where did they come from?

4. Explain the purpose of the evil spirits (verse 14).

5. What happened to the kings of the world (verse 16)?

6. How does one stay awake and keep his garments with him (verse 15)?

William Barclay in *The Daily Study Bible* explains:

> Herodotus tells us . . . that when Cyrus the Persian captured Babylon he actually did so by drying up the Euphrates. The river flows right through the center of Babylon. When Cyrus came to Babylon, her defenses seemed so strong that her capture seemed impossible. Cyrus formed a brilliant plan. He left one section of his army at Babylon and another he took up the river. By a magnificent engineering feat he temporarily deflected the course of the river into a lake. That meant that bit by bit the level of the river dropped, and in the end the channel of the river through Babylon became a dry road, and along the road there was naturally a breach in the defenses, and by that road the Persians gained an entry in the riverbed into Babylon, and the city fell. History knew what the drying up of the river meant for opening a way for invaders.
>
> Here in this vision of the drying up of the Euphrates and the descent of the hordes of the east John was painting a picture of horror both to pagans and to Christians. It was from across the Euphrates that the invasion of the Antichrist was expected.[1]

Three unclean spirits, like frogs, came out of the mouths of the dragon, the beast, and the false prophet. The evil spirits came out of the mouths of evil forces. Their words and their teachings were evil, influencing men and nations against God.

Several times in the Old Testament, frogs are connected with plagues (Exodus 8:5-11; Psalm 78:45; 105:30). Frogs are unclean animals and stand for an unclean influence. Frogs are known for their empty and constant croaking. The sound of the frog makes it the symbol of futile and meaningless speech. To say that frogs came out of the mouths of the dragon (Satan), the beast (the Antichrist), and the false prophet is to say their words were like plagues, they were unclean, they were empty and meaningless, and they were from the power of darkness. The frogs of the Egyptian plague were merely a nuisance; these froglike evil spirits lead men to destruction.

The sixth bowl also sees the assembling of those who would do battle against God, the Almighty. The unholy trinity—the dragon, the beast, and the false prophet—sent forth the spirits to call the kings of the world to battle. The place for their assembly is Har-Magedon (Armageddon, the Mountain of Megiddo; Megiddo means "place of slaugh-

ter"). It is the plain in the Holy Land where Deborah and Barak defeated Sisera and his chariots (Judges 5:19-21) and Gideon overcame the Midianites (chapter 7); where Ahaziah died by the arrows of Jehu (2 Kings 9:27); good Josiah perished in the battle with Pharaoh Neco (2 Kings 23:29-30); and King Saul fought his last battle there (1 Samuel 31). One of the greatest natural battlefields in the world, Har-Magedon is where the Antichrist will gather the world's armies to fight against Jesus Christ (Joel 3; Zechariah 12—14).

In Revelation 16:15, a voice seems to come out of heaven to the Christian community: *Behold, I come like a thief! Blessed is he who stays awake and keeps his clothes with him, so that he may not go naked and be shamefully exposed* (NIV). The only garments that can never be taken away are the garments of righteousness that Jesus himself gives. Those in that day who have those garments will be blessed indeed. This verse encourages believers to not worry about these evil spirits. Just stay spiritually alert and properly clothed (in the white robes of righteousness). Remember, Jesus is coming to take care of you and them.

Why would anyone enter into an alliance with these evil forces to do battle against God? How deceived they must be! There is no chance of victory. Yet everyone who sins and does not repent and turn to God makes exactly the same foolish, eternally damning mistake. That is what this vision is all about. To the wicked, God says, "Repent or perish." To the church He says, "Stay ready and don't worry."

MEMORY CHALLENGE

Write out Psalm 103:15 and 16 from memory.

DAY SIX

Finished

Read Revelation 16:17-21.

1. The last bowl of wrath sets all of nature at war with man. The seventh bowl is poured upon the air, and the act is accompanied by the shout of the Victor, from the throne of the temple in heaven, saying, _____ _____ _____! (TLB).

2. We have read these words before. What caused these words to be spoken by Jesus in John 19:30?

3. List the acts of nature taking place when the seventh bowl was poured out.

4. What comfort are we given in Daniel 12:1?

5. How does Matthew 27:50-51 describe a similar response of nature?

6. Explain what happened to Babylon in Revelation 16:19.

7. Summarize Revelation 16:20-21.

8. Is there hope for us today? Record 2 Chronicles 7:14.

The seventh angel empties the seventh bowl upon the air. From inside the temple (the holy of holies) the divine voice of God is heard declaring, *It is finished!* (TLB). The whole scene is reflecting a sense of total finality. Lightning flashes. Thunder roars. The earth is shaken as it has never been shaken before. That great city of evil, Babylon, is now to drink *the wine of His fierce wrath.* Immediately the very earth is changed. The islands and the mountains disappear. Mighty hailstones, larger than have ever been known before, fall upon men. Blasphemy by tortured human voices is heard. The greater their suffering, the greater their helpless defiance. They have no thought of repentance, whether through God's kindness or the suffering of His judgments.

Having received the mark of the beast themselves, they have assumed his character also. There is indescribable sadness in the words of Revelation 16:9 and 11, *they did not repent . . .*

Psalm 36:1-4 describes the "sinners'" hearts: *Transgression speaks to the ungodly within his heart; there is no fear of God before his eyes. For it flatters him in his own eyes concerning the discovery of iniquity and the hatred of it. The words of his mouth are wickedness and deceit; he has ceased to be wise and to do good. He plans wickedness upon his bed; he sets himself on a path that is not good; he does not despise evil.*

These great and dramatic events are the result of the will of God and occur at His command. In a world that can seem to have no direction and too often appears to have evil leadership throughout many nations, it is important for godly believers to realize that a divine purpose is ruling in the affairs of all people. We are not to think with fear of the coming forces of evil. Rather we are to watch and wear the clean garments of right living, being ready when the Prince of Righteousness shall come.

O LORD, who may abide in Your tent? Who may dwell on Your holy hill? He who walks with integrity, and works righteousness, and speaks truth in his heart (Psalm 15:1-2).

Written by Marie Coody

MEMORY CHALLENGE

Write as much of Psalm 103 as you can, using a separate sheet of paper if necessary.

Revelation

LESSON 17

■ **A Study of Revelation 17**

DAY ONE

Dragon Woman

Read Revelation 17, concentrating on verses 1-5.

Chapters 17 and 18 of Revelation are extensions to the seventh bowl. Chronologically, these chapters are out of order; Revelation 19 should follow 16. But as often is the case in this book, an aside is made to John's vision and another theme is addressed.

Commentators agree that chapter 17 is one of the most difficult chapters of Revelation to interpret. There is general agreement that the main themes are political (discussing the world system that will usher in the end of the world) and religious (revealing a false church that will look very much like Christ's Church).

We will concentrate on the symbolism and spiritual lessons that Revelation 17 teaches. Background information will be given, but political interpretation will be left to the theologians. In the following questions, much of the information is gleaned from Ray C. Stedman's sermon on "The Dragon Lady."[1]

1. What is the character of the Dragon Woman, the great harlot sitting on the red beast?

2. Many clues are given concerning the symbolism of the Dragon Woman and her character. Let's begin examining these by looking at what a harlot is in Scripture. Summarize the following scriptures:

   Ezekiel 16:25-30

   Nahum 3:4

3. A second clue regarding the Dragon Woman is that she has universal influence. What does *sits on many waters* mean? Summarize Revelation 17:15.

4. If the Dragon Woman is seated on the beast, what must be their relationship?

5. Another clue concerning our harlot is her dress and adornment. Summarize this and write what this represents financially.

6. Describe the cup the Dragon Woman holds. Then contrast this with the bowl in Revelation 5:8.

MEMORY CHALLENGE

Psalm 103:17

But the lovingkindness of the LORD is from everlasting to everlasting on those who fear Him, and His righteousness to children's children.

7. As the last clue to symbolism of the Dragon Woman, give her name and what the country in her name represents. If you cannot remember, look back to past lessons.

8. In reading about the Dragon Woman, does the Holy Spirit bring any spiritual lesson to your mind?

In Revelation 17:1, John is told that he will be shown the judgment of the great harlot who sits on many waters. Her influence is worldwide, meaning whatever she represents is everywhere. She has peddled it with nations and kings and common people. Her fare is immorality.

She is a liar, a cheat, and an unfaithful, deceitful woman who sold her soul to the devil and began to sell evil. She has been unfaithful to God by running after other gods including lust, greed, power, influence, and idolatry. As we have studied in past lessons, when a people or nation are unfaithful to God, they are compared to prostitutes. Hosea, a minor prophet of Israel and Judah, prophesied to the people about immorality. *When the LORD first spoke through Hosea, the LORD said to Hosea, "Go, take to yourself a wife of harlotry, and have children of harlotry; for the land commits flagrant harlotry, forsaking the LORD"* (Hosea 1:2). What did this mean? God's chosen people were worshiping other gods. They were not following His law and were committing all sorts of immoralities and sin. They were to be the children of God and the future bride of the Lamb of God. They were to be pure and keep themselves from immorality so they would be worthy to be wed to the Lamb. What righteous man wants to be wed to a prostitute? One of pure character wants to be partnered with another of holy character. But the Dragon Woman represents those who choose sin instead.

Eugene Peterson states that "whoredom is sex connected with money. Worship under the aspect of the great Whore is the commercialization of our great need and deep desire for meaning, love, and salvation. The promise of success, ecstasy, and meaning that we can get for a price is Whoreworship. It is the diabolical inversion of 'You are bought with a price,' to 'I can get it for you wholesale.'"[2]

The Dragon Woman is the mother of all prostitutes. She is the top of her class; the villain of all villains. Her name is written on her forehead, for in the brothels of ancient Rome, this was how prostitutes were identified. Outwardly she is beautiful. She wears the colors of the wealthy in the ancient world and is adorned with jewels. Her seduction of men is very tempting. The Dragon Woman has charm galore. Only the steadfast will avoid her immorality.

So she [a prostitute] seduced him with her pretty speech, her coaxing and her wheedling, until he yielded to her. He couldn't resist her flattery. He followed her as an ox going to the butcher, or as a stag that is trapped, waiting to be killed with an arrow through its heart. He was as a bird flying into a snare, not knowing the fate awaiting it there.

Listen to me, young men, and not only listen but obey; don't let your desires get out of hand; don't let yourself think about her. Don't go near her; stay away from where she walks, lest she tempt you and seduce you. For she has been the ruin of multitudes—a vast host of men have been her victims. If you want to find the road to hell, look for her house (Proverbs 7:21-27, TLB).

The Dragon Woman has only prepared the outside of her cup. She is beautiful outside, but evil through and through. Jesus said in Luke 11:39-41, *I know you Pharisees burnish the surface of your cups and plates so they sparkle in the sun, but I also know your insides are maggoty with greed and secret evil. Stupid Pharisees! Didn't the One who made the outside also make the inside? Turn both your pockets and your hearts inside out* (TM). Outward appearance means nothing if the inside of our being is corrupt. This behavior of the religious leaders of His day, the Pharisees, so infuriated Christ that He followed these words with the seven woes He pronounced on them.

The Dragon Woman represents the corporate evil of all times—the love of what physically, emotionally, and sexually satisfies instead of purity and holiness to our Creator. We understand the Dragon Woman because she is evident everywhere in our culture. We worship money, status, power, fame, sex, image, materialism, entertainment, and pleasures of all sorts, thinking this is the key to happiness. Maybe we worship all this in the name of happiness itself. But we know the end of the story and that all this will never truly satisfy. Just as the Dragon Woman is doomed, so are we if we turn our eyes from the Author and Finisher of our Faith.

There is great warning here, for anything that resembles the Dragon Woman is a danger to us. Anything that causes us to love anything more than God is immorality and idolatry. Remember, it all looks good on the outside and is very tempting, but there is no substance to it. It is like eating marshmallows and whipped cream for supper. Nothing there will sustain.

The rest of the warning is that evil looks so good we often do not recognize it for what it is. We may say we love God and put Him first, but in reality be following the Dragon Woman. This is why it is vital to daily spend time in the Word and prayer and humbling ourselves before the convicting Holy Spirit. This aids us in staying aware of our sin and keeping free of the evil pull of our culture. It keeps us alert, for the Dragon Woman warns us she will even be present in the church.

Beware of the Dragon Woman, for her end is destruction and her doom is sealed.

DAY TWO

Dumbfounded

Read Revelation 17:6-7.

1. The *New American Standard* translation of Revelation 17:6 says that John *wondered greatly* about the Dragon Woman. Record similar phrases from the same verse using two other translations.

2. If we know that the Dragon Woman represents immorality, why do you think John is dumbfounded at the sight of her?

3. What did the messenger angel tell John that God held against the church at Thyatira? Summarize Revelation 2:20-21.

4. Was Jezebel a part of the church at Thyatira? How do people survive in church if they are immoral? Think of as many ways as possible.

5. Has anyone in Bible history appeared to look holy while holding to evil? Read the story of Ananias and Sapphira in Acts 5:1-11, and summarize it.

6. Record Acts 5:11.

7. Jezebel, Ananias, and Sapphira were all church people who chose evil while trying to appear good. How does this principle relate to John being dumbfounded at the Dragon Woman?

Are you understanding by now that John is amazed, dumbfounded, and marveling at the fact that the Dragon Woman is connected with evil because he believed her to be good? Commentators seem to think that the Dragon Woman was a religious institution of the day that appeared so good but was really corrupt. Certainly we see this theme in other Scriptures. For some reason, the church at Thyatira had not thrown Jezebel out even though she was immoral. Ananias and Sapphira wanted to be a part of the Early Church, yet also still wanted to be able to lie. The Pharisees found their traditions and man-made interpretations of the law more important than following God himself or recognizing the Messiah He sent for them. The people of Israel were defeated by the Philistines in 1 Samuel 4 because they were being led by the corrupt priests Hophni and Phinehas, the two sons of Eli. They went out with the ark of the covenant before them without consulting God. They were well known for their evil practices in and out of the Temple, yet they were the priests.

Maybe we always want to believe that our religious institutions are pure and holy. Or maybe the immoral are just exceptionally skilled at looking good. Whatever the reason, John was dumbfounded that what he thought was good turned out to be evil. Haven't we been surprised at some in our day? Whoever would have thought that Jim Bakker or Jimmy Swaggert would fall due to immorality? Do you know of a man or woman who was thought to be a believer but was embarrassed by an affair, tax evasion, business fraud, gambling addiction, homosexuality, or pornography? Unfortunately, we each know of far too many people in these circumstances.

In today's portion of Scripture, John may also be dumbfounded at the institution itself. In other words, the entire religious organization that we all believe to be good may actually be evil. The Dragon Woman does not just represent individuals but a group of some sort.

The best illustration may be the idea of the United States as a Christian nation. We were founded on Christian principles by godly men. We put God at the head of our nation and in times of need go to our knees in prayer. We care for the unfortunate of the world; those torn by war, poverty, disease, earthquake, and other disasters. We philosophize and weep and proclaim how to make it better. Surely we are the "good guys."

But when Israel allowed the evil that is rampant in our country today, God always punished them. They lost wars and their crops failed. Their nation was overrun and cities destroyed while the population was murdered or carried off as slaves. They lost their place of worship and country and children. God did not tolerate their evil. They were not really "good guys" any more than we are.

Whatever this religious institution is that dumbfounded John, we know he was fooled. But God was not fooled—and as always, revealed truth. John so sought the mind and heart of God that this deep and mysterious truth was revealed to him. May truth be revealed to us because we truly seek to know.

MEMORY CHALLENGE

Who experiences the loving-kindness of the Lord?

Doom of Duo

Read Revelation 17:8-10.

1. Who is the second half of the duo with the Dragon Woman?

2. Summarize what is said in these verses regarding the beast.

3. Summarize other verses from Revelation regarding this beast.

   Revelation 11:7

   Revelation 13:1-3 and 14

   Revelation 19:19-20

4. As a review of the cause of the doom of the duo, summarize Deuteronomy 9:4:

   Record Colossians 3:5-6:

5. Verse 8 helps us to explain today's scripture. Complete the phrase, *And those who dwell on the* _____ _____ _____.

The seven heads are believed to represent mountains. Some commentators believe the seven heads represent the completeness of evil. In the ancient world, especially in Egypt, Babylon, and Sumeria, a seven-headed monster represented evil. In order to overcome the monster, each of the seven heads had to be killed. At the Oriental Institute at the University of Chicago, there is a cylinder seal that has an imprint of soldiers one by one killing these seven heads. It is an ancient work of art.

Both mountains and horns stand for authority or power in the Old Testament. If we would ask people from the first century who this passage describes when seven hills and seven kings are mentioned, they would immediately say, "Rome." This was common knowledge in their culture. This is probably the reason most commentators interpret this scripture as the second fall of the Roman Empire.

What caused the first fall of the Roman Empire? Many factors contribute to the crumbling of a great society. The gap between the rich and the poor in their culture widened, and unemployment ran rampant. Conflicts among leaders became great, and often there were civil wars after the death of a leader. The empire was so large that central authority in Rome could not hold it together. Revolts from the outskirts kept the army tied up. Taxes were raised to cover the costs for the huge empire, which led to an economic slump and inflation. Lastly, the population decreased due to drought and crop failure, along with plagues. This also created a problem in the army where there were not enough soldiers. The government forced men into military service.

These were the outward factors, but there were inward reasons also. Power and wealth were often pursued at any cost in Roman culture. The wealthy indulged in entertainment and food. Theater, games at the Colosseum, and discussions of philosophies filled the days for the rich. Eating disorders probably began in Ancient Rome. Sexual sins were common. Homosexuality was rampant, as was heterosexual sex outside of marriage. Abortion was as frequent as was the killing of unwanted infants after birth. Slavery was a necessity to run wealthy households. Women were not treated as equals, yet they created further problems by being so demanding of their rights. Finally, the persecution of Christians cannot be ignored. They were one of the Roman's main sources of entertainment in the Colosseum games where they fought gladiators, were in chariot races, or were fed to the wild animals. The Roman Empire was decidedly immoral and corrupt.

Historians tell us that history repeats itself. So does Revelation. Whether or not this passage actually refers to Rome or truly is a mystery is not the point. The point is that evil, corruption, and sin will always fall. God's plan cannot be thwarted by humanity. But humankind can be wise and learn lessons from history. What have we learned today?

To whom does God's righteousness extend?

Destruction

Read Revelation 17:11-13.

Verses 11 and 12 of Revelation, chapter 17, are most often interpreted politically. Seven to eight, a common concept in the Early Church, means a whole. The beast *which was* means he was alive before he received the fatal wound. *Is not* could mean when he was dead or appeared dead from the wound or that he has no power with believers. *Is* refers to the one last battle in which the beast will be engaged. Reading Daniel 7:24 helps explain verse 12 a bit more.

1. According to verse 13, what is the purpose of these political figures?

2. Part of the reason God's chosen people, the children of Israel, missed the Messiah was that they thought He would be a political figure. What was the golden age of Israel politically, and who did they think the Messiah would be like? Refer to 1 Samuel 16:1, 12-13.

3. Summarize the following prophecies regarding the Messiah.

   Isaiah 9:6-7

   Isaiah 42:1-4

   Jeremiah 23:5-6

   Daniel 7:13-14

4. If you did not have the hindsight to know who Jesus was, would you interpret these scriptures religiously, politically, or spiritually? Why?

5. What were some specific reasons the Pharisees thought Jesus was not the Messiah? Give the answer from the following passages.

   Matthew 9:11

   Matthew 12:2

   Mark 7:5

   Luke 5:20-21

   Luke 7:39

   John 7:43-49

6. Jesus gave the Pharisees so much evidence with His life, yet they still missed Him. List possible reasons the Pharisees had no insight about Jesus being the Messiah.

The Pharisees were convinced that the Messiah was to be a political figure. David was the most respected king of Israel and ruled during their golden age. Surely the Messiah would be even greater than he. The Messiah would come and lead the people as a great military leader. God would go out with the armies, and all of Israel's enemies would be defeated. Then Israel would no longer be an occupied nation but would overthrow the Roman government and once again be a politically powered nation. When peace reigned, the Messiah would be king of Israel and rule with justice and equity and righteousness. He would be wise, wealthy, and a worshiper of the Lord God.

Unfortunately, many of the scriptures that the Pharisees interpreted politically, God intended spiritually. Christ's kingdom was not to be of this earth, as He told Pilate shortly before His crucifixion. His kingdom was of heaven and was available to men on earth. The Messiah came to be our Savior from sin and eternal damnation. He came to include everyone whether Jew or Gentile, Israelite or Roman, Pharisee or nonreligious. His purpose was to save people's souls, not the nation of Israel politically. The Pharisees could not accept this. They had an elaborate concept of what the Messiah would be like. This man Jesus simply did not fit. When they continued to butt their heads against evidence that He was the Son of God, the Messiah, they could not be deterred. They did not want their concept of political deliverance to be wrong, so they clung to it tenaciously. It led to their spiritual destruction.

This is a great personal fear in interpreting today's verses politically. It seems that God's Word centers on spiritual things and that the political issues serve only to enhance the spiritual. When political interpretations have been made in the past, they caused the most religious people of that day to miss the spiritual. The very thing the Pharisees claimed to be most important in their lives, serving God, became exactly the opposite. The Pharisees became the enemies of God and His Son, the Messiah. Their political interpretation of Scripture became their destruction. Surely this is a warning to be careful about elaborate concepts that we are certain are correct. Maybe a wiser approach would be great familiarity with the information, leaving the interpreting to the Holy Spirit when the time comes for the interpretation to be needed. Some caution about elaborate interpretations might be useful.

Lord, we don't want to be so sure we know all the answers that we miss You! Keep our minds and hearts open for what You want to teach us in Your timing.

MEMORY CHALLENGE

How would you explain loving-kindness?

DAY FIVE

Devoted Ones

Read Revelation 17:14.

1. Why will the Lamb overcome those who wage war against Him?

2. Record the following scriptures.

    1 Timothy 6:15

    Revelation 19:16

3. Who are those that are with the Lamb?

4. The devoted ones are the called and chosen and faithful. Let's examine what each of these mean by summarizing the following scriptures.

    The Called

        Ephesians 4:1-3

        2 Timothy 1:9

    The Chosen

        Deuteronomy 7:6

        Psalm 4:3

        John 15:16

The Faithful

Luke 19:17

1 Timothy 1:12

5. Record 1 Thessalonians 5:24.

6. Write your own definition of a devoted one, and give a personal example if possible.

We are called to be Jesus' disciples, chosen to do God's will, and to be faithful in obedience.

As Jesus was walking by the Sea of Galilee, He saw two brothers, Simon who was called Peter, and Andrew his brother, casting a net into the sea; for they were fishermen. And He said to them, "Follow Me, and I will make you fishers of men." Immediately they left their nets and followed Him (Matthew 4:18-20). Peter and Andrew had been in the crowds that had followed Jesus, listening to His teaching. They believed this man and thought Him to be one of God. So when He said to them, *Follow Me*, they knew it was to be His disciples. Wherever Jesus went, they would go with Him, for they had placed their lives in His hands. He would be the leader, and they would be the followers. Jesus would teach them what it meant to live in the kingdom of God. They were the called. They became disciples.

In the Upper Room after Jesus' ascension, the apostles decided to choose one to replace Judas who had betrayed Jesus. They nominated two men and cast lots. The lot fell to Matthias, and he was chosen as one of the apostles. He was chosen to be numbered with those whose lifework was to do God's will. These 12 were dedicated to following closely the commandments of God and what Jesus had taught them. They knew their role was to spread the gospel to the whole world and to lead others to salvation in Jesus Christ. To be obedient children and witnesses to salvation was the will of God for the chosen.

Then the LORD saw that the wickedness of man was great on the earth, and that every intent of the thoughts of his heart was only evil continually. The LORD was sorry that He had made man on the earth, and He was grieved in His heart. . . . But Noah found favor in the eyes of the LORD (Genesis 6:5-6, 8). Only Noah was faithful. *Noah was a righteous man, blameless in his time; Noah walked with God* (verse 9b). To be faithful to God, one must obey all that God commands him. In Noah's day that was whatever the Lord told one to do. Even things as outrageous as building a huge ark with no body of water close by. In our day it means obeying the Scriptures, for that is God's Word, and following whatever the Holy Spirit may tell us personally to do. Obedience is faithfulness; the faithful are obedient.

We are the called and chosen and faithful. We are called to be disciples of Jesus; each of us being chosen to do His will. We are the faithful and obedient. This makes us devoted. Devoted to God, our Father, the Creator, Author and Finisher of our faith. Are you devoted? Open your heart, listen to what the Lord may have to say to you right now and respond to Him, determined to be devoted.

MEMORY CHALLENGE

Fill in the blanks:

But the _____ of the LORD

is from _____ to

_____ on those who

_____ Him, and His

_____ to children's

_____.

                                                        Psalm 103:17

Divided

Read Revelation 17:15-18.

1. Who will hate the Dragon Woman?

2. What will they do to her?

3. On which side of good and evil is the Dragon Woman, the beast, and the 10 horns or kings?

4. What did Jesus say about a kingdom divided against itself? Summarize Mark 3:24-26.

5. What is the opposite of divided?

6. Evil may get along for a time, but in the end will always be divided, for it is too self-serving to cooperate for the unity of the group. What do the Scriptures teach us about division and unity among believers?

   Psalm 133:1

   Ephesians 4:1-3

   1 Peter 3:8

"United we stand, divided we fall" is not merely a flip statement. Where there is division, there is always strife. If the strife becomes too great, any hope for unity is lost. In any organization, the division weakens it. The organization will only be strong through unity.

But in this sinful world, there are so many self-interests that unity is often hard to achieve. If everyone is looking out for Number 1, who will be looking out for the organization? The Dragon Woman, the beast, and the 10 kings all had their own ideas of what they wanted to happen. We may be sure it was all guided by self-interest. In the end, what will corrupt their powerful group is division among themselves. They will not be able to get along, agree, or compromise in order to maintain their power. They will fall by ingrown fighting.

Jesus craved just the opposite for us. In Christ's last verbal prayer that we have recorded for His disciples, He prayed for unity. *The glory which You have given Me I have given to them, that they may be one, just as We are one; I in them and You in Me, that they may be perfected in unity* (John 17:22-23). Even when we have differences as believers, we are to find a way to agree, to unite, for that is the only way we will survive. Division will shatter our existence. *There may be no division in the body, but that the members may have the same care for one another* (1 Corinthians 12:25).

The purpose of our lives is to love and glorify God by following His Son, Jesus, as our Savior and to bring others to know Him. Whether believers or unbelievers, God will direct us to do as He pleases. This was in today's scripture in Revelation 17:17 where it says, *God has put it in their hearts to execute His purpose.* This meant for the evil crowd division. But for the righteous crowd this means unity. They are self-serving. We are God-serving. Therefore, we do not seek our own will and desires, but those of God. As God directs His will for His believers, it would be the same. So believers would have this same purpose and be unified in it.

Sometimes how we interpret God's will or carry it out may take on different meanings to different people. Probably there are a few differences worth fighting over. But mostly it will be more important to agree so we may be unified. In Revelation, we see the end to the reign of evil. We learn an incredibly valuable lesson when we understand that it is finally destroyed from within. Internal division causes evil to lose. May unity cause believers to win.

Written by Linda Shaw

Write out this week's memory verse.

Revelation

LESSON 18

■ A Study of Revelation 18

DAY ONE

Doom

Read Revelation 18:1-3.

Revelation 16, 17, and 18 tell the story of the doom and to-tal destruction of Babylon. Chapter 16 relates the judgment of the seven bowls of God's wrath. In chapter 17, religious and ecclesiastical Babylon is destroyed. Chapter 18 tells us of the destruction of the commercial and government systems. Babylon, the harlot of chapter 17, will be destroyed by the kings of the earth (17:16); commercial Babylon will be destroyed by the cataclysmic judgment of God.

1. What is announced by the angel in Revelation 14:8?

2. Revelation 18:1-2 tell of another angel coming down from heaven and repeating the message. How does John describe this angel?

3. What will dwell in the ruins of Babylon and be imprisoned there?

4. What have the nations, the kings, and the merchants done to incur the wrath of God?

Announcing the fall and total destruction of Babylon is an angel of power and authority so great that he illuminates the earth with his glory. Where will this center of governmental power and commercial wealth be? Bible scholars disagree. Some believe it will be Rome; New York is the suggestion of a few because the UN is headquartered there. Possibly, a city will be rebuilt on or near the site of ancient Babylon on the banks of the Euphrates River (in modern Iraq).

5. Summarize the following verses describing the awe-some judgments of God against Babylon.

Jeremiah 51:26

Jeremiah 51:37

Although ancient Babylon lies in ruins today, the prophe-sied total destruction and absence of human life has not yet been completely fulfilled. Parts of the ancient city have been found in at least six cities, including Baghdad. Hillah, a 20-minute walk from Babylon, was built almost entirely from its ruins. Wandering shepherds sometimes graze their sheep in this area. The Iraqi leadership have indicated their desire to rebuild the city, and spy satellites and flights have shown increased activity in the area. Beneath the sands of Iraq lies potentially great wealth and world power in the vast resources of oil.

The importance of this passage to us, however, is not whether Babylon is symbolic of a satanic system of gov-ernment and political power or a literal rebuilding of the

---

MEMORY CHALLENGE

Psalm 103:18

To those who keep His covenant and remember His precepts to do them.

ancient city as a center of power and luxury. God is giving warning that the wicked but enticing Babylon and its system will reap His wrath and judgment and is doomed to be utterly destroyed.

The religious, economic, and political power of the world will be concentrated in Babylon. "[Babylon] will be toasted around the globe as the enlightened, liberated city, hidebound by none of the foolish fads of prudish religious quacks," states John Phillips. "The rulers of the earth will be captivated by the prospect of getting rich through her trade."[1] Her wealth and luxury will entice many into forsaking God and committing spiritual adultery by turning to the worship of materialism. God's authority will be denied, morality and ethics forgotten or ignored, in the quest for material wealth by any means.

When religious Babylon is destroyed, political Babylon will also come to an end. God will deliver His judgment, and Babylon will fall. Babylon represents the purpose of Satan, a kingdom of men under the puppet rule of the Antichrist, in opposition to God and His plan of salvation through Jesus Christ. As a world political federation, it denies Christ the right to reign; as a religious system, it denies the authority of Christ. It is the center of idolatry, the occult, demonism, and all false religion.

The spirit of Babylon is present and growing stronger in the world today. Materialism is prevalent in our society. Followers of Christ must stay alert to resist the seductive temptation to place the desire for material possessions, and the power they bring, above their love for Christ and His kingdom. *The Reader's Digest Great Encyclopedic Dictionary* defines materialism as "the doctrine that physical well being and material possessions constitute the highest good," and as "undue regard for the material rather than the spiritual . . . [aspect] of life."[2]

6. What does God's Word say concerning materialism? Summarize these verses:

   Psalm 37:16, 18

   Proverbs 11:4

   Matthew 6:19-21

7. Read Matthew 19:20-26. What does Jesus tell the rich young man to do? How did the man respond?

8. What was the warning of Jesus found in Luke 12:15?

9. Read Luke 12:22-34. What does Jesus encourage us to seek rather than things?

Wealth and material possessions are not evil in themselves but must not be given "undue regard" lest they become the gods we serve rather than God Almighty. God must have first place in our lives. He will not tolerate the worship of the gods of the world.

Depart!

Read Revelation 18:4-5.

1. John *heard another voice from heaven.* What did the voice command and to whom was the command addressed (verse 4)?

2. What did the heavenly voice say concerning the sins of Babylon?

From earliest recorded Scripture, the Bible reflects a negative view of Babylon. The name of the city was called Babel (Hebrew for Babylon) *because there the Lord confused the language of the whole earth* and the people were *scattered . . . abroad over the face of the whole earth* (Genesis 11:9). The tower of Babel (verses 1-9) represents the excesses of human ambition and arrogance that eventually resulted in the name of Babylon being used to represent great sin and wickedness (Revelation 17:5). Here John shows us a picture of the sins of Babylon heaping up, one after another, until the pile reaches heaven itself. He uses a word that literally means "glued" together to form a heap.

The people of God are called to *come out* of Babylon for two reasons: (1) that they *will not participate in her sins,* and (2) that they will not *receive of her plagues* (punishments). This call for God's people to *come out* is sounded throughout Hebrew history. Sometimes, God has actually meant for His people to physically remove themselves from sinful surroundings.

3. Read the following verses and identify the persons who are being told to depart and the reason why.

   Genesis 19:15

   Jeremiah 50:4-5, 8-10

   Zechariah 2:6-7, 9

Matthew 2:13-16

In His letters to the churches in Revelation 2 and 3, Christ warns the churches against being seduced by the deceit of Satan and becoming worldly-minded. In Revelation 18:4, God calls His people to *come out* of Babylon as the end of the Tribulation nears. And in love and mercy, God is calling out His people today. In fact, the Greek word for "church" is *ecclesia,* which means "an assembly of called-out ones." He is not calling us to remove ourselves physically from society to live in an isolated and segregated community of believers, but to resist the spirit of the world, the secular and materialistic values and morals so pervasive in our society. "It is not a question of retiring from the world; it is a question of living differently within the world."[1] Jesus has called us out, not to segregation (although we may have to remove ourselves physically from certain situations), but to separation from sin that we might take the message of salvation (Matthew 28:19-20) and be salt and light (5:13-16) to a sinful world.

During the Tribulation, the temptation to compromise and come to terms with the sins of Babylon will be intense. Persecution would then cease, and luxury and comfort would replace deprivation. In today's society, we are enticed and tempted to compromise with the values and morals of the sinful world in which we live. "Wherever there are idolatry, prostitution, self-glorification, self-sufficiency, pride, complacency, reliance on luxury and wealth, avoidance of suffering, violence against life, there is Babylon. Christians are to separate themselves ideologically and, if necessary, physically from all the forms of Babylon."[2]

4. As followers of Christ and people of God, we must not indulge the old sinful nature, but must walk in accordance with the Spirit (Romans 8:12-14; Galatians 5:16).

   Summarize:

   Romans 12:2

   2 Corinthians 6:14

   Galatians 6:7-8

Ephesians 5:11

God warns us that if we do not avoid the contamination of sin in our lives, we will participate in the doom of Babylon, the punishment of the judgment of God. God will not be mocked! John Phillips, in *Exploring Revelation*, reminds us that heaven may seem silent and indifferent to the corruption of the world, God may seem deaf and blind, and evil men may seem to be getting away with their sins, but God will not forget. He will judge and punish the sin and the sinner (2 Thessalonians 1:6-9). (See also 1 Samuel 2:10; 2 Peter 3:7; Jude 14-15; Revelation 19:2.)[3]

How may we separate ourselves from sin and walk in the Spirit? God has given us His three Rs: (1) Recognize the sin in our lives as sin, and deal with it honestly; sin must not be rationalized or excused. (2) Repent—Confess our sins before God (1 John 1:9) and ask for forgiveness. (3) Radical obedience—We must faithfully and obediently resist the temptations of sin and walk in the light shed across our path as we listen to God's voice through daily study of His Word and in prayer.

5. If you are comfortable doing so, share with your group ways in which God has led you to separate yourself in radical obedience from worldly values and moral standards (example: entertainment, television, reading materials, honesty, compromise, sexuality, etc.).

> *Depart, depart, go out from there!*
> *Touch no unclean thing!*
> *Come out from it and be pure,*
> *. . . for the LORD will go before you,*
> *the God of Israel will be your rear guard.*
> Isaiah 52:11-12, NIV

Praise the Lord!

Fill in the blanks:

But the _____ *of the* LORD *is from*

_____ *to* _____ *on*

those who _____ *Him, and His*

_____ *to* _____

_____, *to those who* _____ *His*

_____ *and* _____ *His*

_____ *to do them.*

Psalm 103:17-18

Destruction

Read Revelation 18:6-8 with Isaiah 47:7-11.

1. How will Babylon be paid back for her deeds?

2. The voice from heaven accuses Babylon of two sins. What are they (verse 7)?

3. Of what does she boast?

4. Isaiah's lament for Babylon is found in Isaiah 47:7-11. List the similar condemnations expressed here by Isaiah and by John in Revelation 18:6-8.

In Revelation 18:4-5, the voice from heaven addressed the people of God, calling them out from their evil surroundings. In verses 6-8, the instructions are not to men, but to God's divine instrument of justice (possibly the angel of verse 1). Vengeance belongs to God, not men (Romans 12:17-21).

5. Read Hebrews 10:29-31. According to verse 29, who deserves the most severe punishment?

6. Hebrews 10:31 says, *It is a terrifying thing to fall into the hands of the living God.* Record the words of the Lord in verse 30.

Doubling the punishment was not unusual in Jewish law; anyone responsible for loss or damage had to repay doubly (Exodus 22:4, 7, 9; Isaiah 40:2; Jeremiah 16:18). Babylon is to be repaid for what she has done to the saints of God, for her many excesses, and for her rejection of, and opposition to, God and the blood sacrifice of His Son, Jesus Christ.

For a while, the plans and dreams of Satan will seem to have succeeded. There will be a one-world government, a universal apostate religion of works and denial of grace, extreme luxury and sensuality, and worship of Satan and his beast. Already, there have been great strides toward one global policy, economic system and religion, even one global language, as well as a revival of the spirit of Babylon.

Suddenly and without warning, it will end. It has become a popular refrain that a loving and merciful God will not punish the sinner. That is a lie of Satan! The righteousness of a holy God demands justice (Revelation 19:2). Babylon's punishment will fit her sins (Obadiah 15; Colossians 3:25; Revelation 16:5-7). It is not revenge, but requital; she will be repaid for her crimes. God's wrath will be related to her sin (Romans 1:18, 28-32) and her persistent refusal to repent (Romans 2:5-6; Hebrews 12:16-17; Revelation 2:5).

The spirit that characterizes Babylon is one of opulent luxury, arrogance, pride, sensuality, self-deception, self-indulgence, self-sufficiency, self-glorification, and blind optimism. Her great prosperity blinds her to the coming judgment of God; prophets of doom are no doubt mocked and ridiculed. Babylon has everything the heart could desire and expects it to last forever; she has no need for God.

However, *pride goes before destruction* (Proverbs 16:18). We are living in danger of allowing the sins of pride and arrogance into our lives. Pride and arrogance lead to the sins of self-indulgence and self-sufficiency. When we no longer feel the need for God to direct our lives and provide for our needs, we commit the sin of self-glorification. We become our own god. Nothing brings more condemnation from God than the sin of pride (Isaiah 3:16-26; Ezekiel 28:5-8, 17).

7. Summarize these verses:

   Psalm 101:5

   Proverbs 16:5

   Isaiah 13:11

   Jeremiah 50:32

Revelation 3:17

8. Name the four plagues God will inflict upon Babylon (Revelation 18:8).

In just one day (Isaiah 47:9; 1 Thessalonians 5:3), Babylon will receive God's judgment and His justice and will experience the very things she has avoided—pestilence, mourning, and famine. Fire will bring total destruction, and the arrogant "queen" will be able to do nothing to stop it. Even the great secular power of the world's mightiest kingdom is frail and impotent compared to the mighty power of God!

9. Challenge Question: Read Psalm 37 and summarize the chapter in one sentence.

MEMORY CHALLENGE

On a separate piece of paper, write Psalm 103:17-18 several times.

Despair

Read Revelation 18:9-19.

Despair: "to lose or abandon hope; utter hopelessness and discouragement. Despair is the utter abandonment of hope that leaves the mind apathetic or numb."[1]

1. Name the three groups that will weep and mourn in despair over the destruction of Babylon the great.

2. Where will each of these groups be during the destruction of Babylon?

3. Of what acts are the kings of the earth accused?

4. Why do the merchants of the earth weep and mourn?

5. Why do all the seafarers (shipmasters, passengers, sailors) weep and mourn?

6. How long did God's judgment against Babylon take?

7. Challenge: Read Ezekiel 26 and 27 and be aware of the similarities in the lament over Tyre and the lament over Babylon.

William Barclay says, "In the time when John was writing a kind of insanity of wanton extravagance, to which it is very difficult to find any parallel in history, had invaded Rome,"[2] an almost desperate competition in ostentation and gluttony. The luxury of Babylon no doubt would have been identified with the luxurious excesses of Rome in the minds of the persecuted Christians to whom John was writing. Whether ancient Babylon will be rebuilt, or whether Babylon is symbolic of Rome in the end time, or whether it merely represents a worldwide system of government and religion, there will be wealth beyond anything with which we can relate.

The apostle John tells of three groups who stand in the distance and weep and mourn over the destruction of Babylon—the kings, the merchants, and all that go to sea. This is not silent weeping but loud wailing and beating their breasts in grief. There is no attempt to help the doomed city, only purely selfish sorrow that the market that had provided their great wealth is gone. In each case, the lament is for themselves; they mourn over lost profits and customers and fear of what will happen to them. History tells us that a society that is built on luxury, moral decay and wantonness, pride, or a disregard for human life and personality (slavery) is always doomed. Babylon is laid waste, utterly destroyed, in despair; they have no hope in the face of disaster (Job 8:13; 27:8-9).

8. Summarize Job 31:24-25, 28.

John knew that there was enormous economic pressure on these first-century Christians to participate in Roman culture and its values in order to enjoy its material benefits. In the future kingdom ruled over by the Antichrist, there will be even greater economic pressure to conform and accept his mark in order to buy or sell or conduct any business (Revelation 13:16-17). Faithful Christians will face persecution and death. There will be great temptation to compromise one's faith.

9. Material prosperity and secular power are highly prized in our world today. Is your heart set on earthly things or on the things of God and His kingdom? How do you view the luxuries of this world? What would be your reaction if it all went up in smoke? Would you be in despair? Summarize these passages.

Matthew 6:24-25, 33

Philippians 3:18-20

Hope: "An attitude toward the future, an assurance that what is bad will pass and that what is good will be preserved. . . . Hope is a theme in many places in the Bible even when specific words for hope are not used. . . . There are promises from God to which one clings as one faces the unknown and often forbidding future. . . . But hope is also an inner sense of confidence in God, a serenity despite terrible present circumstances."[3]

10. Briefly summarize what these verses say concerning hope:

Psalm 31:24

Psalm 33:18-22

Psalm 71:5, 14

Romans 5:2, 5

Romans 15:13

1 Timothy 1:1

Titus 1:2

1 Peter 3:15

   In the [New Testament] hope is shown springing from the Resurrection of Jesus (1 Peter 1:3). This hope became a characteristic quality of the early Christians in sharp contrast to the pervading despair of the pagan world. Paul listed hope as one of the three basic qualities of the Christian (1 Corinthians 13:13) and declared that the hope of salvation was a helmet (1 Thessalonians 5:8). He said that men are saved by hope (Romans 8:24 [25], 35-39) and described God as the "God of hope" (Romans 15:13). In Colossians Paul writes of the "hope which is laid up for you in heaven" (1:5), mentions the "hope of the

gospel" (1:23) and declares that "Christ in you" is the "hope of glory" (1:27).[4]

Do you have this blessed hope in Christ Jesus? God does not want you to be in despair. *For you know that God paid a ransom to save you from the empty life you inherited from your ancestors. . . . He paid for you with the precious lifeblood of Christ, the sinless, spotless Lamb of God. . . . And he did this for you. Through Christ you have come to trust in God. And because God raised Christ from the dead and gave him great glory, your faith and hope can be placed confidently in God* (1 Peter 1:18-21, NLT).

MEMORY CHALLENGE

What has the Lord promised to those who fear Him?

What has He promised to those who keep His covenant and remember His precepts to do them?

Delight

Read Revelation 18:20, with Psalm 9.

The Reader's Digest Great Encyclopedic Dictionary defines "delight" as "to take great pleasure; rejoice."[1]

1. To whom were given instructions to rejoice over the destruction of Babylon?

2. Why were they instructed to rejoice?

3. Even as the kings, merchants, and seafarers wail and mourn their lament over the destruction of Babylon and the loss of her pleasures and wealth, heaven and the saints and apostles and prophets are told to rejoice. The call to rejoice over the destruction of the city might seem harsh, especially in the light of scriptural appeals to love our enemies. Summarize:

   Proverbs 24:17

   Luke 6:27-28

   Romans 12:14

Jesus forgave those who condemned Him to death (Luke 23:34) as did Stephen (Acts 7:59-60), even as their sentences were being carried out. Yet, here, heaven, the saints, the apostles, the prophets—all are told to rejoice. Could this be a contradiction in Scripture? No, definitely not!

Babylon's sins have become so large and so vile that even a long-suffering, merciful God must administer justice. The citizens of Babylon have been given many reminders of the awesome power of God and of His wrath toward sin but have steadfastly refused to repent. And this is not a call to be vindictive or vengeful; it is not rejoicing over the agony of Babylon's fall. This is a call to rejoice because their faithfulness in God has been vindicated. It is the re-

joicing of faith in believing that God would keep His promises and that His faithful followers would be on the winning side. John and his readers had staked their very lives on the truths of the Christian faith. People around the world today are trusting God and staking their lives on His Word, facing enmity, persecution, and death, out of the deep conviction that someday evil will be defeated and righteousness will triumph. Isaiah, Jeremiah, Ezekiel, Daniel, and other prophets have long waited to see their prophecies fulfilled. Now judgment has come—not vengeance, but justice.

4. Reread Psalm 9, a hymn of thanksgiving for God's justice. Summarize these verses that tell of rejoicing because of God's justice.

   1 Chronicles 16:31-33, 35

   Psalm 18:46-49

   Psalm 68:1-3

   Isaiah 61:7-8

5. As Christians, we should love our enemies and pray for them, but we should also rejoice over every demonstration of God's victorious power in our world. Think of some recent victories for the kingdom of God that have caused you to rejoice—and share them with your group.

6. In 1 Thessalonians 5:16 Paul tells us to *rejoice always*, and in Philippians 4:4 to *rejoice in the Lord always*. Read these verses and list the reason given for rejoicing.

   Psalm 5:11

   Psalm 13:5; 35:9

   Psalm 28:7

Luke 10:20

Luke 15:10

7. Summarize the promises found in Isaiah 25:8-9.

To the degree that you share the sufferings of Christ, keep on rejoicing, so that also at the revelation of His glory, you may rejoice with exultation (1 Peter 4:13).

MEMORY CHALLENGE

Review Psalm 108:17. Who will receive His righteousness to children's children?

Desolation

Read Revelation 18:21-24.

1. What did the strong angel do?

2. How did the angel compare his action with Babylon?

3. List those things that will no longer be heard or found in the doomed city.

4. How were all the nations deceived?

5. What was found in Babylon?

A strong angel *took up a stone like a great millstone and threw it into the sea.* Alan Johnson describes this giant boulder as being "four to five feet in diameter, one foot thick and weighing thousands of pounds."[1] This action symbolizes the violent destruction and disappearance of Babylon. When this huge stone hits the water, circles of disturbance move far outward as the sea closes over the stone. It disappears suddenly, violently, and completely, never to be seen again. The waters become still, and it is as if it had never existed. This recalls the action of Jeremiah when he commanded Seraiah to weight with a stone his book of prophecies of the calamity that would come upon Babylon and to throw it into the Euphrates River (Jeremiah 51:60-64).

6. Record the prophecy of Jeremiah found in Jeremiah 51:62.

The angel describes the desolation of this once great city. Revelation 18:9-19 describes the loss of her trade, which had brought such great wealth and luxury and the weeping and mourning of those who profited by it. Verses 22-23 describe the desolation within the city itself:

Never again will there be any sound of music and re-
    joicing.
Never again will there be any sound of a craftsman
    plying his trade.
Never again will there be any sound of domestic activ-
    ity (housewives grinding grain).
Never again will there be lights in the streets or in
    homes or offices.
Never again will there be any sound of a bride or
    bridegroom rejoicing; even love will die.
(Jerusalem: Jeremiah 16:9; 25:10; Tyre: Ezekiel 26:13)[2]

All normal life will cease; the desolation in Babylon will be
complete.

The angel then emphasizes the evils of Babylon. The
wealthy merchants had not only sent their goods throughout all the earth but also exported the spirit of Babylon—
the worship of wealth and luxury and material things, the
wanton wickedness and the rejection of the true God and
worship of the beast. They had deceived the nations with all
manner of evils, sorceries, astrology, and all sorts of magic.

Babylon was guilty of the slaying of prophets and saints
and all those who have been martyred because of their
faithfulness in following God (Revelation 6:9-10; 11:7;
13:15). Their blood was on her hands (16:6; 17:6; 19:2).
Babylon the great was held accountable for her blood-
guilt. The doom and desolation of Babylon was justified!

If you were to be here at the time of the destruction of
Babylon, would you be among the weepers and mourners
or among those who rejoice? If you have not accepted Jesus Christ as your Savior and followed Him in radical obedience, if your life seems desolate, dark, and empty, read 1
John 1:5-10. Confess your sins and accept His forgiveness
(1 John 1:9) that your *joy may be made complete* (verse 4).

Written by Helen Silvey

MEMORY CHALLENGE

Be able to repeat Psalm 103:17-18 from memory and say it
with your small group.

FOOTNOTE

In 1788, more than 200 years ago, Edward Gibbon wrote *The Decline
and Fall of the Roman Empire.* He gave five basic reasons why that
great civilization died:
1. The undermining of the dignity and sanctity of the home, which is
   the basis for human society.
2. Higher and higher taxes; the spending of public money for free bread
   and circuses for the populace.
3. The mad craze for pleasure; sports becoming every year more exciting, more brutal, more immoral.
4. The building of great armaments when the real enemy was within—
   the decay of individual responsibility.
5. The decay of religion; faith fading into mere form, losing touch with
   life, losing power to guide the people.

We have been warned that history repeats itself. We can see these five
things becoming ever more present in today's culture. These are the
things that will bring down the Babylon of tomorrow. Will the contem-
porary individual, the home and the family, and our nation be destroyed
as well?

*[If] My people who are called by My name humble themselves and
pray and seek My face and turn from their wicked ways, then I will
hear from heaven, will forgive their sin and will heal their land (2
Chronicles 7:14).*

Revelation

LESSON 19

■ A Study of Revelation 19

DAY ONE

Righteous and True

Read Revelation 19, concentrating on verses 1-4.

1. Which two groups are worshiping in these four verses?

2. Record the phrases of praise spoken in verses 1 and 3.

3. The word "hallelujah" means "_____ _____ _____." (Look up the first sentence of Psalms 111, 112, and 113 to find the answer.) Give three to five reasons from Psalm 111 to say "hallelujah!"

4. We should praise God for His attributes. List an attribute or characteristic of God given in each of the following scriptures.

    2 Samuel 7:22

    Psalm 139:7

    Isaiah 40:28

Jeremiah 32:17

Romans 11:33

1 John 3:20

5. What is the reason the 24 elders and four living creatures are lifting praise to God?

6. Read the following scriptures and tell why God's judgments are righteous and true.

    Psalm 12:6-7

    Psalm 139:1-3

MEMORY CHALLENGE

Psalm 103:19

The LORD has established His throne in the heavens, and His sovereignty rules over all.

Romans 16:27

As we come to Revelation 19, Babylon has just fallen. There will be no more song, no more craft, no more marriage, no more industry, and no more light in Babylon. The third woe has just been completed and one might expect unhappiness and sorrow, but God's concluding words are of salvation, not judgment. Twenty-four times in the Old Testament the words *hallelujah* or *praise the Lord* are used. Maybe in this acclamation session each of the 24 elders repeated one of those hallelujahs from the Old Testament! But now the word *hallelujah* is being used for the first time in the New Testament, acknowledging the power and reign of the eternal God.

Praise is about lifting up the attributes of God. Each attribute of God should have a response from the human heart. For example, Revelation 19:1 says, *Hallelujah! Salvation and glory and power belong to our God.* To salvation the believer would respond with gratitude. To God's glory the believer would respond with reverence. To the power of God a believer would respond with trust. True praise brings a loving response in the heart of the believer to the attributes of God.

Revelation 19 also reminds us that the inescapable consequence of sin is judgment. This is a moral law that can no more be broken than the law of gravity can be defied. The harlot committed the greatest of sins when she taught others to sin or led them into sin. Revelation 18 speaks of the judgment of Babylon and the harlot. God's judgments are righteous and true. He knows the inmost thoughts and desires of man, so He is able to judge with truth and righteousness. God is a pure and wise judge.[1] We tend to be fearful when being judged by someone who is unfair. Yet we have no reason to be afraid of God's judgment. However, we must remember that we will be judged according to our deeds and the condition of our heart. As we keep these righteous and true, we need have no fear in God's judgment.

Praise, honor, and glory are due the righteous and true God, for His concluding Word is not of judgment but salvation. Hallelujah!

Reigns! Celebrate!

Read Revelation 19:5-6.

1. What did the voice from the throne say to do?

2. How did the voice of the great multitude respond?

3. Record phrases from the following scriptures regarding the fact that God reigns.

    Psalm 47:8

    Psalm 93:1

    Psalm 97:1

    Psalm 146:10

    1 Corinthians 15:25

4. What should be our response to the reign of God?

    Exodus 18:9

    2 Samuel 6:5

Nehemiah 8:9-12

Psalm 126:1-3

1 Peter 4:13

5. When an event occurs in your life or the life of a loved one that is a victory for Christ's cause, do you celebrate? How?

For responsible people, tasks and problems can quickly fill up a day, a week, a lifetime. When something good happens that God has provided in our lives, it is easy to quickly go back to the tasks and problems. But what about taking time to celebrate?

In our culture, we celebrate designated holidays throughout the year. What a wonderful diversion from work and great opportunity to be with family and friends. But often this becomes a habit, and we do not really stop to contemplate why we are celebrating. In the United States even Christmas, the holiday commemorating the birth of our Savior, has become so commercial and busy that finding time to dwell on the incredible gift of God's Son is difficult.

When God provides victory and blessings in our lives, it seems that it would be pleasing to Him if we took time to appreciate it. The father of the prodigal son knew how to do this! When his son returned home and confessed his sin, the father had the best robe put on him, along with a ring on his hand and sandals on his feet. They killed the fatted calf and began to eat and be merry, for the lost son was found! (Luke 15). It was time for a celebration!

Don't you think the Heavenly Father was greatly enjoying that from up above? God had wrought a miracle in the life of a young man. They were right to take time to rejoice!

When we celebrate on such occasions, we are really honoring God for His goodness in our lives. His blessings to us are being celebrated! When we gripe and worry over problems, we show our fear that God is not in control. When we celebrate, we give our praise that He is!

The end of the Book of Revelation speaks of celebrating. The first seven verses of Revelation 19 have to do with celebration. Chapter 21 rejoices in the descriptions of the new heaven, new earth, and new Jerusalem. It tells us that *God Himself will be among them [His people], and He will wipe away every tear from their eyes; and there will no longer be any death; there will no longer be any mourning, or crying, or pain* (verses 3-4). Revelation 22 tells us of the River of Life coming from the throne of God and the tree of life. We are told, *The Spirit and the bride say, "Come." And let the one who hears say, "Come." And let the one who is thirsty come; let the one who wishes take the water of life without cost* (verse 17). Sounds like a celebration!

6. Be creative in thinking of new ways to celebrate or to begin to celebrate when God blesses you with victories. Jot down a few ideas to share with your group.

Life is busy. Life is hard. But God is good! Take time to celebrate!

MEMORY CHALLENGE

Where has the Lord established His throne?

DAY THREE

Resplendent Wedding

Read Revelation 19:7-10.

1. Who is getting married?

2. To clarify further, look up the following scriptures and write how the Lamb or bridegroom was identified.

   Isaiah 54:5

   Mark 2:18-19

   John 3:28-30

   2 Corinthians 11:2

   Ephesians 5:25

3. Summarize Hosea 2:19-20 to help you understand the purpose of this marriage.

4. According to Hosea 2:20, what should be our response?

5. In Revelation 19:8, what does the fine linen worn by the bride represent?

6. The following parables have to do with weddings. Select and record a spiritual principle from each one.

   Matthew 22:1-14

   Matthew 25:1-13

7. Record the testimony of Jesus in Revelation 19:10.

When a wedding of a well-matched couple is to take place, there is much joy and excitement. Finally, each has found his or her partner, and they commit to spend a lifetime together maturing in their relationship. Family members on both sides are thrilled, and proud parents can now see their job as complete.

The preparation and expense of such a wedding can be amazing. Much time is spent arranging for a florist, caterer, minister, singers, travel for family members, and honeymoon just to name a few! Hours are spent planning, shopping, deciding, and practicing even for a short ceremony. Why? It is part of our tradition and culture to make a wedding an important and once-in-a-lifetime event. Girls dream about it from the time they are little!

The wedding of Revelation 19 has been expected for ages. Throughout the Old and New Testaments, the prophecy of the wedding of the Lamb is foretold. Isaiah 54:5 says, *For your husband is your Maker, whose name is the LORD of hosts* meaning God's plan was for Him to be wed to the nation of Israel. Unfortunately, this could only be done if Israel was a holy nation. Since Israel was repeatedly disobedient, this plan failed. Israel's faithlessness meant the marriage was unfulfilled.

The New Testament speaks of the marriage of the Lamb to the Bride who is the "Church." Israel has been replaced by any who are willing to accept Christ as their Savior and live in obedience to Him. That is who the "Church" is. Those who are pure and holy and righteous become the Bride.

This brings us to the symbolism for the clothing of the Bride. *Bright* is the description of glorification. Surely we, as mere humans, will be glorified to become the Bride of the Lamb! *Clean* reflects purity, loyalty, and faithfulness. The Bride is given the garment of the righteous, but she has had to make herself ready to receive it. She has made herself ready by her righteous acts. The preparation for this wedding is much different from material and traditional plans. The preparation for this Bride is to be pure and holy.

Revelation is full of talk of this marriage, for this is the completion of God's plan for humankind on earth. He always intended to have a holy people set apart to whom He could become a husband. Finally, all the conditions are right for this to happen. It is a glorious wedding; the happening of the ages! The fulfillment of a match well made, permeated with holiness and righteousness and purity. What a wedding that will be! May we not only be invited but be there clothed *in fine linen, bright and clean!*

MEMORY CHALLENGE

Over whom does the Lord's sovereignty rule?

DAY FOUR

Reigning Ruler

Read Revelation 19:11-16.

1. What are the four names given in this passage to the rider on the white horse?

2. Give a description of the rider.

3. One title for the rider of the white horse could be Reigning Ruler. What are some other titles that could be given Him?

4. What are the three things the Reigning Ruler will do according to verse 15? Match the answer with the following scriptures.

   Psalm 2:9

   Isaiah 11:4

   Isaiah 63:1-6

5. Was this Mighty Warrior's battle and victory foretold in Scripture? Summarize Zechariah 14:3-4.

6. This description of the Reigning Ruler is a bringing together of many descriptions of Christ in Revelation. Give the phrase from each of the following scriptures.

   Revelation:

   1:14

2:18

2:27

3:14

6:2

14:19-20

15:5

17:14

Are you beginning to understand that this passage describing the Reigning Ruler, the Conquering Christ, is a description of the Second Coming? The war warrants no description, for its outcome is already determined. It is the rider who is the center of attention, the only focus. He is now the Victor, fulfilling every purpose that is always righteousness.

Roman generals always rode on white horses, so it is not surprising that this is the picture John saw. The rider having eyes that are a flame of fire cast Him as the Mighty Conqueror. A king of John's day wore the crowns of the nations he had conquered, so in his view, the Ruler of the World would wear the crown of every nation, people, and place. This showed His power and authority as King of Kings.

His robe dipped in blood has been argued over by commentators. Some believe this is His own blood from His sacrifice on the Cross. Others believe since He came from heaven to earth, it was the blood of the saints. Finally, some suggest it is the blood of His enemies whom He has conquered. Maybe it is the blood of all three, for certainly His blood has mingled with that of all humankind.

He is followed by a heavenly army, possibly angels or maybe the saints gone on before. They, too, ride white horses, symbolizing purity and victory. With the sword of His mouth He will smite the nations, although we are told of no physical battle. He will rule with an iron scepter as foretold in Psalm 2:9, showing that His rule must be absolute in our hearts. Finally in that day on earth, this rider on the white horse will tread the winepress of the fierce wrath of God, the Almighty.

The Reigning Ruler will have the names Faithful and True, the Word of God and the King of Kings and Lord of Lords. And He will have a name written on Him that no one will know but himself. Commentators again disagree over where the unknown name (verse 12) will be found on Him, although the most popular location is His thigh. Apparently, this was common for warriors and chosen for its visibility. But why can't we know this name? Maybe because until Christ returns *we see in a mirror dimly, but then face to face* (1 Corinthians 13:12).

Can you image the majesty with which Christ will return? Can you feel the finality of it? Can you sense the power, honor, and glory? Christ will be the Reigning Ruler, the Conquering Christ for once and evermore! Doesn't it just make you want to shout "glory"? What a day that will be! We look forward to the day when Christ returns to claim His kingdom come on earth. Praise His name!

MEMORY CHALLENGE

Do you think it is a coincidence that the memory verse for this week is the exact theme as today's lesson. You might want to discuss this in your group and then say the memory verse aloud with them.

Results

Read Revelation 19:17-19.

1. What did the angel say to the birds?

2. Who assembled for this battle?

3. Summarize further prophecy related to this passage from Ezekiel 39:17-20.

4. Did Christ speak of this in the New Testament? Record Matthew 24:28.

5. Where is this battle to take place? See Zechariah 14:3-4.

6. What do we call this battle? Refer to Revelation 16:13-16.

During the Super Bowl one year, it became clear late in the fourth quarter which team would win. Before the end of the game, those team members began to don hats that read Super Bowl Champs. How did they know ahead of time that they would win?

In that situation I'm sure both sides had such hats printed up. Only the winners took them out of the trunk and began to wear them. But in today's scripture, without a doubt, the results are in before the battle is fought! All the birds of the world are called to enjoy a feast of the bodies of the evil, for they will be defeated. Death will be no respecter of persons. Nationality, status, strength, or ability won't be an issue. Those who are evil will go down. Before the battle is fought, the results are in!

As a prelude to the battle, an angel standing in the sun cries out for all the birds in midheaven to come to the

biggest feast for fowl in the history of the world. Birds of prey include eagles, falcons, condors, osprey, kites, owls, buzzards, hawks, and vultures. These are helpful creatures to the environment in that they hunt animals that eat stored grain, such as rabbits, mice, and rats. Some birds of prey eat bones, hair, and fur as well as flesh. Most have a well-developed sense of smell along with excellent eyesight to spot prey from great heights in the air. The birds will swoop down on their prey as fast as 200 miles per hour and with jagged, strong claws and powerful legs grab creatures. Their sharp bill, often with a hooklike beak, will tear off the flesh of the animal victims. Birds of prey are found worldwide and can soar or glide for long distances. Condors, for example, will soar for an hour only flapping their wings once.

Now try to picture all the birds of the world from midheaven being called to clean up the mess! That is a feast for fowl with results! Hasn't God planned for every detail? As we look back at history we see He has always been faithful, true, and accurate. The results are in. God's people win!

MEMORY CHALLENGE

Fill in the blanks:

The LORD has _____ His

_____ in the _____, and His

_____ rules over all.

Psalm 103:19

DAY SIX

Rebuked!

Read Revelation 19:20-21.

1. In verse 19, the beast, kings of the earth, and their armies are assembled to make war with the rider on the white horse. What happens in this battle in verses 20-21?

2. Reexamine verses 15 and 21 and tell by what method God's enemies were destroyed.

3. Record John 1:1, emphasizing the last four words.

4. Summarize the part of the following scriptures that show the power of God's Word.

   Isaiah 11:4

   2 Thessalonians 2:8

   Hebrews 4:12

   2 Peter 3:5-7

5. Summarize what happened in the following stories when Christ spoke.

   Matthew 8:28-32

   Mark 4:37-39

John 11:43-44

John 18:4-6

6. Which of the above scriptures uses the title of today's lesson in it?

As the armies of good and evil gather for Armageddon, the anticipation of a mighty battle comes to mind. The day dawns with a clear, blue sky, but the atmosphere is ominous. Someone fires the first shot while planes buzz overhead, dropping bombs and paratroopers. Men crawl into position on their bellies while others peer over foxholes. Explosions blaze in the already bright sky, and screams of pain are part of the noise. Military strategies and sophisticated weaponry abound. The stench of violence, blood, injury, and death irritate the nostrils. This is war.

But upon closer examination of God's Word, we realize it may not happen this way at all. Troops will gather, but as Martin Luther says in his great hymn, "A Mighty Fortress Is Our God," when Christ meets Satan and his forces, "one little word shall fell him."

In other words, the Conquering Christ, the Reigning Ruler, will speak a word and the war will be over. No fighting, no shooting, no contest. Remember how surprised we were by the Israeli-Iraqi conflict in 1969? The world was braced for a Middle East war that would affect the rest of the world for months, maybe years. Instead, it was over in six days because Israel was so powerful. Armageddon will be even shorter. Once the rider on the white horse speaks, the enemy will be defeated and the war will be over. Now that's rebuked!

At a word from God, the world was created and later flooded and again restored. At a word from God, His Son became flesh and dwelt among us. At a word from Jesus, blind men regained their sight, deaf men received their hearing, and lame men jumped for joy. Simply by stating that He was the one they were seeking, the soldiers in the Garden of Gethsemane fell back. Jesus could have walked right through those troops just on His own spoken word. But His time had not come for that, and His capture had another purpose. However, in Revelation 19, all is fulfilled for Christ to take His place on the throne of the earth as the Conquering Christ, the Reigning Ruler. When that time comes, all He has to do is speak the word.

What a mighty God we serve! He is powerful beyond compare! Let His Word have power in your heart and life.

Father, bless the name of Your Son. He is powerful beyond description! May we be careful to follow Your words well and not let a single one fall to the ground unattended. Amen.

Written by Linda Shaw

MEMORY CHALLENGE

Fill in the blanks for Psalm 103:1-19:

Bless the LORD, O my _____, and all that is within me, _____ His holy _____. Bless the _____, O my soul, and _____ none of His _____; who _____ all your _____, who _____ all your _____; who _____ your life from the _____, who _____ you with _____ and _____; who _____ your years with good _____, so that your _____ is renewed like the _____. The LORD _____ righteous _____ and _____ for all who are _____. He made known _____ _____ to Moses, His _____ to the sons of _____. The LORD is _____ and _____, slow to _____ and abounding in _____. He will not always _____ with us, nor will He keep His _____ forever. He has not _____

with us according to our _____, nor _____ us according to our _____. For as high as the _____ are above the earth, so great is His _____ toward those who _____ Him. As far as the _____ is from the _____, so far has He removed our _____ from us. Just as a _____ has compassion on his _____, so the LORD has _____ on those who _____ Him. For He Himself knows our _____; He is mindful that we are but _____. As for man, his _____ are like _____; as a _____ of the field, so he _____. When the _____ has passed over it, it is _____ _____. And its place _____ it no longer. But the _____ of the LORD is from _____ to _____ on those who _____ Him, and His _____ to children's _____, to those who keep His _____ and _____ His _____ to do them. The LORD has _____ His throne in the _____, and His _____ rules over all.

Psalm 103:1-19

Revelation

LESSON 20

■ A Study of Revelation 20

DAY ONE

Satan Is Bound

Read Revelation 20:1-3.

1. What was in the hand of the angel John saw coming down from heaven?

2. In this passage of Scripture, what names are given to the one the angel bound for 1,000 years?

3. Summarize Revelation 20:3.

4. Describe what the "abyss" brings to your mind.

5. In the story of the Gerasene demonic in Luke 8:26-31, what request did the demons make of Jesus?

6. Refer back to Revelation 9:1-3. What took place when the angel opened the bottomless pit (abyss)?

William Barclay describes the abyss as a "vast subterranean cavern beneath the earth, sometimes where all the dead went, sometimes the place where special sinners were kept awaiting punishment. It was reached by a funnel or channel or chasm reaching down into the earth. It was the chasm which the angel locked in order to keep the devil in the abyss. It was the abyss which the demons feared most of all."[1]

Satan is not bound in chains for punishment (that occurs in Revelation 20:10). Satan is bound in chains to keep him from deceiving the nations. An angel from heaven has thrown Satan into the abyss, shut it, sealed it over him, and he cannot deceive the nations again for 1,000 years, when he must be released for a short time.

Scripture makes many references to the devil (God's chief opponent) and Satan (God's adversary):

Titles:

Abaddon—Revelation 9:11

Accuser—Revelation 12:10

Adversary—1 Peter 5:8

Angel of the abyss—Revelation 9:11

Apollyon—Revelation 9:11

Beelzebub—Matthew 12:24

Belial—2 Corinthians 6:15

God of this world—2 Corinthians 4:4

Murderer—John 8:44

Serpent of old—Revelation 20:2

Ruler of demons—Matthew 12:24

MEMORY CHALLENGE

Psalm 103:20

*Bless the LORD, you His angels,
mighty in strength, who perform His word,
obeying the voice of His word!*

Prince of the power of the air—Ephesians 2:2

Ruler of the world—John 14:30

World forces of darkness—Ephesians 6:12

Evil one—Matthew 13:19

Origin:

Heart lifted up in pride—Isaiah 14:12-20

Blameless until sin came—Ezekiel 28:14-19

Greatest of fallen angels—Revelation 12:7-9

Father of lies—John 8:44

Designs:

To undo God's work—Mark 4:15

To make men turn away from God—Job 2:4-5

Instigates evil—John 13:2, 27

To secure men's worship—Luke 4:6-8 and 2 Thessalonians 2:3-4

Method:

Disguises himself—2 Corinthians 11:14

Insinuates doubt—Genesis 3:1

Misuses Scripture—Matthew 4:6

Uses schemes—2 Corinthians 2:11

Afflicts believers—Luke 13:16

Character:

Crafty—Genesis 3:1; 2 Corinthians 11:3

Slanderous—Job 1:9

Fierce—Luke 8:29

Deceitful—2 Corinthians 11:4

Powerful—Ephesians 2:2

Conceited—1 Timothy 3:6

Cowardly—James 4:7

Evil—1 John 2:13

Power over the wicked:

They are his children—Acts 13:10; 1 John 3:10

They do his will—John 8:44

He possesses—Luke 22:3

He blinds—2 Corinthians 4:4

He deceives—Revelation 20:7-8

He terrorizes—1 Samuel 16:14

They are punished with him—Matthew 25:41

Power over God's people:

Tempt—1 Chronicles 21:1

Afflict—Job 2:7

Accuse—Zechariah 3:1

Sift—Luke 22:31

Deceive—2 Corinthians 11:3

Disguises—2 Corinthians 11:14-15

Believer's power over:

Watch against—2 Corinthians 2:11

Fight against—Ephesians 6:11-16

Resist—James 4:7; 1 Peter 5:9

Overcome—1 John 2:13; Revelation 12:10-11

Judgment upon:

Bound—Mark 3:27

Cast out—John 12:31

Judged—John 16:11

Crushed—Romans 16:20

Assigned to hell—Matthew 25:41

Christ's triumph over:

Predicted—Genesis 3:15

Portrayed—Matthew 4:1-11

Proclaimed—Luke 10:18

Carefully considering these descriptive references to Satan, think of the pests that can disrupt a well-planned family outing. Hoping to enjoy a picnic, we can be annoyed by flies, mosquitoes, gnats, and ants. The mosquitoes want to feed on us; they, with the flies and gnats, fly around us disturbing a peaceful setting; the ants and flies want to eat our food. They will disrupt fun and fellowship until necessary measures are taken to get rid of them. On a much larger scale, Satan is a great annoyance and pest. First Peter 5:8-9 (NIV) tells us, *Be self-controlled and alert. Your enemy the devil prowls around like a roaring lion looking for someone to devour. Resist him, standing firm in the faith.*

No one wants any of his names.

His origin came as a result of his sin against God in heaven.

His design is to keep us from God.

His method is 100 percent deceit.

His character is evil.

He rules the unrepentant with lies and fear.

As we use our power to overcome him, our lives are blessed and joyous. Christ has triumphed over him and has given believers power to resist him and make him flee. Eternal judgment is coming. He cannot stand against the blood of the Lamb Christ Jesus and the word of our testimony.

Father, thank You for the gift of discernment. May we develop a greater capacity to recognize Satan as he comes against us to deceive and defeat us. Thank You that the power, through the blood of Jesus, is available to fight, resist, and overcome all of his evil schemes and afflictions.

Martyrs Resurrected

Read Revelation 20:4.

1. John saw thrones, and sitting on them were those who had been given the right to judge. Record the words of Jesus to His disciples in Matthew 19:28.

2. Record Paul's phrases from 1 Corinthians 6:2-3 that tell of others who will judge the world.

3. Revelation 2:26-27 includes others that will rule. Who are they?

4. Why had martyrs been beheaded?

5. The martyrs had been resurrected and were alive again. What would they be doing the next 1,000 years?

Those who have been loyal to Christ are to receive the privilege of judgment. In this world the Christian may be a man under persecution and under the judgment of men; in the world to come the roles will be reversed, and those who thought they were the judging authority will be the ones who are being judged.

Christians from across the United States were gathered in Tulsa in late April, 1999 for the national conference of Voice of the Martyrs, whose U.S. headquarters are in Bartlesville, OK. Speakers—to protect their identity were known only by their first name—were mostly victims of religious persecution. Those attending were VOM volunteers and supporters.

VOM works worldwide to help the suffering persecuted Christians in Sudan, Iran, Saudi Arabia, Vietnam, Ethiopia, China and elsewhere. In Sudan tens of thousands of Africans are enslaved by Islamic terrorists and thugs. Christians are imprisoned in Iran and Saudi Arabia.

Saudi Arabia is so rabidly Islamic that Swiss Air planes cannot fly there because the airline's logo is a cross. No planes are allowed to fly over Mecca because their shadow forms a cross. This is certainly within the country's rights, but charging foreigners with blasphemy because they are Christians is not.

"Pastor Wally" was a Filipino working in the Saudi ministry of defense in 1992. He was a leader in the underground house church movement in Saudi. Spies were sent into the meetings to gather information. Arrests followed. Wally—sold out by a spy for 30,000 Riyals—was arrested "not for crimes but because of my beliefs."

Placed in a cell that was three feet by four feet, Wally found it impossible to sleep. He was forced to witness the flogging of other prisoners after the noon prayers. At midnight he heard the cries of torture.

Then Wally was tortured. He was beat up for 210 minutes straight. The injuries to his feet made it impossible to walk. Lesser men with lesser faith would have taken the easy way out and pretended to renounce their Christianity. Wally would not.

"I prayed that God would send angels, and He did. They picked me up. I began to appreciate what it is like to share the suffering of my Savior." A wave of the Holy Spirit not only comforted Wally, the Holy Spirit empowered him to forgive his captors.

"I felt mercy toward them. They did not know what they were doing. Instead of bitterness and hatred, I felt such love for my tormentors."

Asked repeatedly to admit he believed Islam would fail, he at first answered: "Partly." The reply only intensified the beatings and left Wally stricken. So he answered yes and prepared for the worst. "I began to hear angels singing, found myself blinded by a pure white light and felt hands touching my body. Suddenly, I felt the sweetest touch on my face. I knew it was Jesus. The next day they were surprised to find me alive and with no marks of torture on my body."

You may accept or dismiss Wally's encounter with angels. But you cannot ignore the persecution each day in this world of thousands like him. Many victims will tell you that when the persecution reached a zenith, something supernatural occurred. A flood of comfort rushed in. Pain lifted. Hate turned to love.

Wally was convicted of blasphemy and sentenced to death. Hours before his scheduled execution, international pressure reached the highest levels of the Saudi government. His death sentence was not only commuted, he was eventually allowed to return to the Philippines.

Was his faith unwavering through all this? No. When his young daughter was allowed to visit, she didn't recognize her father at first, so altered was his appearance by one torture session. "I came very close to raising my fist to heaven when my daughter didn't recognize me. But then she did and she told me not to cry, that Jesus loved me."

Wally bargained with God, reminding Him of the story of Paul and Silas and prison walls coming down. "I said, 'God, Paul's story is my story'" and cited examples of how his life and ministry had paralleled the trials of the great apostle. "Within seconds, God gave me a wonderful response. He said, 'You are not Paul. You are Wally.'"

Wally walked away from certain death, but many are not so blessed. The Tulsa conference was dedicated to their lives and to their martyrdom. Two thousand years after the original Christian martyr, Jesus Christ, the killing continues.

"There is a price to pay in order for others to be free," Wally said. "Pain and suffering define the Christian life. The body of Christ needs to awaken to the pain others are feeling. Would you spend just 10 minutes a day praying for our persecuted brothers and sisters?"[1]

✳ ✳ ✳

Will you join others in W.O.W. who have committed to pray for Christian brothers and sisters who are suffering persecution?

For more information, contact:
    The Voice of the Martyrs
    P.O. Box 443
    Bartlesville, OK 74005-0443
    Web site: www.persecution.com

MEMORY CHALLENGE

This verse was true in the life of Pastor Wally in our lesson today.

_____ the LORD, you His _____, mighty

in strength, who perform _____ _____, obey-

ing the voice of _____ _____!
                                                        Psalm 103:20

The Millennium

Read Revelation 20:5-6.

1. The thousand years are often referred to as the millennium (Latin for "one thousand"). Summarize Revelation 20:5.

2. How does John 5:28-29 explain resurrection for believers and unbelievers?

3. What are the blessings for the ones who have a part in the first resurrection (Revelation 20:6)?

4. How are Christians identified in 1 Peter 2:9-10?

5. How does Revelation 21:8 describe the second death mentioned in Revelation 20:6?

6. Record the warnings in these scriptures:

    Psalm 95:8

    Hebrews 2:1

Just how and when the millennium, or thousand-year reign of Christ, takes place is understood differently among Christian scholars. There are three major positions on this issue: (1) Postmillennialism, popular in the early 20th century, sees Christ's return after the millennium, which has been brought about by the spread of the Church through the power of the Holy Spirit. (2) Premillennialism places Christ's second coming before the millennium, which is established by the supernatural intervention of God in Christ. Jesus himself will usher in the reign of 1,000 years on earth. (3) Amillennialism rejects the idea of any literal reign of Christ on earth for 1,000 years. They see the millennium as a figurative expression of the accomplishment of God's Word to Israel, fulfilled in the Church. These different views about millennium need not cause division and controversy in the Church, because each one acknowledges what is the most vital to Christianity—Christ will return, defeat Satan, and reign forever. Whatever and whenever the millennium is, Jesus Christ will unite all believers and not let this issue divide us.

Christians hold two basic views concerning the First Resurrection (20:5-6): (1) Some believe the first resurrection is spiritual, and that the 1,000 years (millennium) is our spiritual reign with Christ between His first and second comings because He reigns in our hearts. In this view, the second resurrection is the bodily resurrection of all people for judgment. (2) Others believe the first resurrection occurs after Satan has been bound and cast into the abyss. It is a physical resurrection of believers who then reign with Christ on the earth for the actual 1,000 years. The second resurrection occurs at the end of the millennium (1,000 years) in order to judge unbelievers who have died.

The second death is spiritual death—everlasting separation from God (20:6). Those who have allowed their hearts to be deceived and hardened against God can no longer have any hope.

People with hardened hearts know the truth but resist it and refuse to obey it. They know that God chastens disobedient children, but they almost defy God to act. They think they can sin and get away with it. The first step toward a hard heart is neglect of the Word of God (Hebrews 2:1-4), not taking it seriously. It is either hearing or hardening. Take your choice (Psalm 95:6-11).

Father, break up the hardened ground of every unyielded heart and plant seeds of loving conviction of sin.

MEMORY CHALLENGE

List the three phrases in Psalm 103:20 that describe His angels.

DAY FOUR

Satan Is a Loser

Read Revelation 20:7-9.

1. What will happen after the thousand-year reign of Christ and His saints?

2. How is the abyss described?

3. Satan will go to the four corners of the earth to deceive the nations. What is Satan's goal in gathering people at this time?

4. Are Gog and Magog friends or enemies of God? (Refer to Ezekiel 38:2-3.)

5. John described those who will be deceived by Satan *the number of them is like the sand of the seashore.* What was Satan's battle plan for them in his war against God?

6. How did God defeat the armies of Satan?

7. Why do you think people are so willing to follow a doomed loser like Satan?

8. What can we do to keep from being deceived by Satan?

The battle of Armageddon occurs before the millennium (Revelation 19:19-21) with the Antichrist as the enemy leader. Satan is the leader in this battle after the millennium. Gog and Magog symbolize all the forces of evil, gathered from everywhere, who join together to battle God.

This is not a typical battle where the outcome is in doubt during the heat of the conflict. Actually, there is no conflict. Two mighty forces of evil—those of the Beast (19:19) and of Satan (20:8)—do battle against God. The Bible uses just two verses to describe each battle—the evil Beast (Antichrist) and his forces are captured and thrown into the Lake of Fire (19:20-21), and fire from God consumes Satan and his attacking armies (20:9). For God it is as easy as that. There will be no doubt, no worry, no second thoughts for believers whether they have made the right choice. If you have chosen God, you will experience this tremendous victory with Christ.[1]

9. Write a prayer of thanksgiving to God for His assurance of eternal life with Him because of His defeat of Satan.

MEMORY CHALLENGE

A verse that expresses blessings from angels and relates to Psalm 103:20 is Psalm 91:11-12, *For He will give His angels charge concerning you, to guard you in all your ways. They will bear you up in their hands, that you do not strike your foot against a stone.*

Psalm 103:20

Bless the LORD, _____ _____ _____,

_____ _____ _____, who per-

form His word, _____ _____

_____ of His word!

DAY FIVE

Satan Is Doomed

Read Revelation 20:10.

1. Where was Satan dispatched after his defeat?

2. Who had already been there 1,000 years?

3. What will they experience in the future?

4. How can we draw encouragement from the certainty of Satan's doom?

5. Are you being made more aware of evil in the world as we study the Book of Revelation? Explain.

6. Obedience to God's Word will protect us from the same doom as Satan's. What instruction are we given to guide us in our walk with Him in Matthew 7:13-14?

Satan's power is not eternal—he will meet his doom. He began his evil work in humankind at the beginning (Genesis 3:1-6) and continues it today, but he will be destroyed when he is thrown into the lake of fire. Satan was released from the abyss (the bottomless pit) (20:7), but he will never be released from the lake of fire. He will never be a threat to anyone again.

The Bible records for us the beginning of the world and the end of the world. The story of humanity, from beginning to end—from the fall into sin to the redemption of Christ and God's ultimate victory over evil—is found in the pages of the Bible.

Genesis
    The sun is created.
    Satan is victorious.
    Sin enters the human race.
    People run and hide from God.
    People are cursed.
    Tears are shed, with sorrow for sin.

The Garden and earth are cursed.
The fruit from the tree of life is not to be eaten.
Paradise is lost.
People are doomed to death.

Revelation
The sun is not needed.
Satan is defeated.
Sin is banished.
People are invited to live with God forever.
The curse is removed.
No more sin, no more tears or sorrow.
God's city is glorified, the earth is made new.
God's people may eat from the Tree of Life.
Paradise is regained.
Death is defeated, believers live forever with God.[1]

In Genesis we see an evil, victorious Satan. In Revelation we see he will be in the lake of fire forever. Satan deceived himself and is now deceiving others.

7. Revelation is causing us to see again and again the determination of Satan to defeat us. How can we be strengthened in our fight against him? Summarize:

Zechariah 8:16

Matthew 18:19-20

Romans 12:5

Ephesians 4:22

Would you consider praying with a prayer partner each week? If so, ask God to put you with someone who also wants to pray with another believer and grow in Him. Wait for Him to direct you. It will probably be a person you might not have considered. He knows the one for you. You can begin by sharing a quiet time using *God Calling* (edited by A. J. Russell). Reading his introduction "The Two Listeners" will give you an understanding of the book.

God's way may appear to be a narrow way, but it leads to abundant life. Follow the narrow way; it is not so narrow but that He can walk beside you.

MEMORY CHALLENGE

Review Psalm 103:1-20 in preparation for writing it on Day 6.

DAY SIX

The Final Judgment

Read Revelation 20:11-15.

1. What was the effect of God's presence on *earth and heaven* at the Great White Throne Judgment?

2. Who will be involved in the Final Judgment?

3. Where is God recording what people do in this life?

4. On what basis will people be judged at the end of time?

5. From what diverse places will the dead assemble for the judgment?

6. What will happen to those whose names are not found in the book of life?

7. How does one get his or her name recorded in the book of life?

8. Is there a step you need to take today to ensure that your name is written in the book of life?

9. How can you help someone avoid a future in the lake of fire?

The dead are now judged before the great white throne of God; the throne is white symbolizing the absolute purity of the Judge. Earth and heaven flee away, which tells us it is not a judgment on earth but it is a judgment in eternity. *Heaven and earth will pass away, but My words will not pass away* (Mark 13:31). Heaven and earth were completely destroyed, *no place was found for them* (Revelation 20:11).

All the dead stood before the throne and the books were opened. In the books are recorded the deeds of everyone, good or evil. Report cards from school are insignificant compared to the reports recorded in these books. Every person was judged according to his or her deeds. Deeds reveal what is in the heart. Righteous deeds are done by the power and energy of the Holy Spirit. Other deeds may look good on the outside but inwardly can be tainted by the selfish, self-centered desire for prominence or power, influence or recognition.

The idea here is very simple: a record of all men's deeds is kept by God. The reality is that all through life we are writing our own destiny; we are compiling a story of success or failure in the sight of God; our record will bring us either honor or shame in the presence of God. Every person is the author of his or her own life story. It is not so much that God judges us as it is that we write our own judgment.

The second book is the book of life, which contains the names of those who have put their trust in Christ to save them.

At the time of judgment it is said that the sea will give up its dead. No matter how a person dies, he or she will face punishment or reward.

Death and Hades are thrown into the lake of fire—when God's judgment is finished. The lake of fire is the ultimate destination of everything wicked—Satan, the beast (Antichrist), the false prophet, the demons, death, Hades, and all those whose names are not written in the book of life because they had not placed their faith in Jesus Christ.

The requirement to be allowed entrance into heaven is indicated clearly: having one's name written in the book of life. This means acceptance of Jesus Christ as Savior and Lord. To keep one's name there requires being an overcomer. *He who overcomes will thus be clothed in white garments; and I will not erase his name from the book of life, and I will confess his name before My Father and before His angels* (Revelation 3:5). Ultimately this is the only thing that really matters.

I am standing on the seashore and see a nearby ship spread her white sails to the morning breeze and start for the blue ocean. She's an object of beauty and strength. I watch her until at last she is only a speck of white just where the sea and the sky meet and mingle. Then someone at my side exclaims, "She's gone!"

Gone where? Gone from my sight, that is all. She is just as large in hull and spar as she was when she departed, and just as able to bear her load of living freight to the place of her destination. Her diminished size is in me, not in her.

And just at the moment when someone cries, "She's gone," there are other eyes watching for her arrival, and other voices that take up the glad shout, "There she comes!"

(author unknown)

And that is what dying will be like for those whose names are recorded in the book of life!

Written by Marie Coody

MEMORY CHALLENGE

Write from memory Psalm 103:1-20. Use a separate piece of paper if necessary.

Revelation

LESSON 21

■ **A Study of Revelation 21**

DAY ONE

God's New Creation

Read Revelation 21, concentrating on verses 1-4.

1. How could there be a new heaven and a new earth?

2. Are we lifted up to heaven into the new Jerusalem?

3. Summarize the announcement from verse 3.

4. What will life be like in heaven?

5. Summarize the prophecy of Isaiah 25:8.

6. Personalize Psalm 23 as a prayer.

After the purging of the earth of Satan and his followers, after the judgment upon those who reject Christ and His grace, and after cleansing the earth of the heartache and tears of sickness, sin, death, and the grave, will come a new creation. It is a new creation with a new heaven and a new earth. In it is the new and holy city, the heavenly Jerusalem, and in it is the presence of the dwelling place of God himself.

A "holy" city will be one in which no lie will ever be told, no evil word will ever be spoken, no shady business deal will be discussed, no unclean picture will be seen. It will be holy because everyone in it will be holy.

Revelation 21:2 tells us, *The holy city, new Jerusalem . . . made ready as a bride adorned for her husband.* There is a time in a woman's life when she has a right to be extravagant, one time she prepares herself with the greatest care and dresses as elegantly and beautifully and attractively as she can—the time of her marriage. As a bride adorns herself for her husband, so will God adorn and beautify this city for His loved ones. Think of all the beautiful things in the world God has made—sunsets, mountains, lakes, roses, beautiful trees, snowflakes, clouds, waterfalls. What will a city be like made by the Divine Architect? John 14:2 says, *I go to prepare a place for you.*

God Himself will be among them. In the Garden of Eden Adam and Eve were driven from the immediate, conscious presence of God. In this passage of Revelation 21:1-4, it is being restored. As long as we live on earth we will walk by faith. In the new heavenly Jerusalem we shall actually see God and be with Him in loving fellowship through ceaseless cycles of never-ending ages.

MEMORY CHALLENGE

Psalm 103:21

*Bless the LORD, all you His hosts,
you who serve Him, doing His will.*

Tears, death, sorrow, and pain are all passed away. There are no graves on the hillside of glory and no funeral wreaths on the doors of those mansions in the sky. All of that is gone forever.

No matter what you are going through, it is not the last word—God has written the final chapter, and it is about true fulfillment and eternal joy for those who love Him. We do not know as much as we would like to know, but it is enough that eternity with God will be more wonderful than our human minds can imagine. It will be worth it all.

DAY TWO

Overcomers

Read Revelation 21:5-8.

1. *Faithful and true* (Revelation 21:5) characterizes not only the spoken and written Word but also the Incarnate Word, Jesus Christ. Record Revelation 3:14.

2. What title for Jesus Christ is given in Revelation 21:6?

3. The Alpha and Omega, which are the first and last words of the Greek alphabet, indicate that Christ is before the universe, which was created by Him, and will be at the end of all time, for all things will be completed in Him. Record Romans 11:36.

Just as God finished the work of creation (Genesis 2:1-3) and Jesus finished the work of redemption (John 19:30), so the Trinity will finish the entire plan of salvation by inviting the redeemed into a new creation.

4. Who will inherit God's promised blessings (Revelation 21:7)?

Overcomers are those who *endure to the end* without renouncing Christ (Mark 13:13). They will receive the blessings God promised. Record phrases of promises from these passages:

Revelation 2:7

Revelation 2:11

Revelation 2:17

Revelation 2:26

Revelation 3:5

Revelation 3:12

Revelation 3:21

Those who endure the testing of evil and remain faithful are those whom God will reward.

In verse 8 we read something that we would not expect to find in this description of the Holy City. We are given another reminder of sinners who will not be there but instead *will be in the lake that burns with fire and brimstone, which is the second death.* These are dreadful words. If we accept with gratefulness and thanksgiving the promises of God's Word, we must also believe its solemn warnings.

In this list with the *abominable and murderers and immoral persons and sorcerers and idolaters and all liars* are *the cowardly and unbelieving.* Unbelievers could be morally good people but without faith in Jesus they are hopelessly lost. Is being "cowardly" a sin? Yes. Cowards are not those who are fainthearted in their faith or who sometimes question or doubt. They are those who turn away from God and refuse to accept Him as Savior and then follow Him. They are not brave enough to stand up for Christ; they are not humble enough to accept His authority over their lives.

The destiny of sinners is destruction, not life. They should not respond to cowardice, but faith;
    not unbelief, but truth;
    not murder, but life;
    not immorality, but wholeness;
    not mysticism, but relationship;
    not idols, but encounter with the living God;
    not lying and deception, but the openness of trust.

Do you know anyone who would be included in those referred to in verse 8?

Is God showing you how to help them become those who can be overcomers? Is He urging you to act now?

MEMORY CHALLENGE

Fill in the blanks:

_____ *the* LORD, *all you* _____ _____,
you who _____ *Him, doing His* _____.

                                               Psalm 103:21

DAY THREE

All Believers Welcomed

Read Revelation 21:9-14.

1. *Then one of the seven angels who had the seven bowls full of the seven last plagues came and spoke with me, saying, "Come here, I will show you the bride, the wife of the Lamb"* (Revelation 21:9). How does this verse compare with 17:1?

The great harlot and the pure bride of the Lamb—the sameness of the introduction only serves to accent the extreme contrast between the two visions.

2. There is a symbolic description of the beauty and glory of the Bride of Christ reflected in the imagery of her home—the eternal city of God. With what is the source of brilliance in the Holy City compared (verse 11)?

3. Compare verses 12-13 with Ezekiel 48:30-35. Ezekiel saw a picture of the Holy City, which is an early glimpse of John's vision of the Holy City with its gated walls on each of its four sides. From this passage, list the four sides of the city with the names of the three tribes assigned to each gate in the wall.

This is telling us that although God may be a long time in fulfilling His promises, they will be fulfilled in His timing if men are living in obedience to His Word. Also, His promise will be fulfilled in such a way that no one is neglected; God's concern is for all people as well as the tribes of Israel. The person who turns to God in this world and serves God faithfully here is the man who will spend eternity with His God.

The scripture passage for today contains the description of the New Jerusalem. The most important question we must ask is: what is the theological significance of this part of John's vision? The principal concern of this description is to show that the Christian Church is the true fulfillment of the people of Israel. The vision makes clear that the New Jerusalem will include the original holy history of Israel (David's city, Jerusalem, in the Old Testament) and the expanded Israel of all those who believe in Israel's Messiah (including Gentiles, in the New Testament). The description of the 12 foundations of the temple have inscribed upon them not the names of the tribes of Israel but the names of the 12 apostles of the Lamb, Jesus Christ. The Holy City involves both the old and the new covenants. All of God's people are welcome here, both Jews and Gentiles.

3. What phrases in these passages express His love for all people?

   Matthew 11:28

   John 1:12

   John 17:20-21

   Romans 10:12-13

   Revelation 3:20

Red and yellow, black and white, we are all precious in His sight.

Dear Lord, make us color blind in our relationships with others—just as You are.

Who should bless the Lord?

Measures

Read Revelation 21:15-17.

1. Summarize what is being done in this passage.

2. What are the dimensions of the city?

3. How do you visualize the city?

4. How is the holy of holies (inner sanctuary) described in 1 Kings 6:20?

Carpenters in denim overalls—blue and white stripes or solid denim blue—usually have a Stanley measuring tape hanging from the waist with a carpenter's pencil in the bib of their overalls. The angel measuring the Holy City needs a different method of measuring for a 1,500-square-mile area. Can you create in your thoughts a picture of an angel measuring the city, its gates, and its walls? Verse 17 appears to mean that the angel used ordinary human measures, not some extraordinary measure of his own.

Fifteen hundred miles is the distance between London and Athens, between New York and Houston. A city of this size is too large for the imagination to take in. John is certainly conveying the idea of splendor. And, more importantly, that there is room for all.

The measurements of the Holy City are symbolic of a place that will hold all God's people. Given in cubits, these measurements are all multiples of 12. Twelve is the number for God's people—there were 12 tribes in Israel and 12 apostles who started the Church. The walls are 144 cubits across (216 feet across), there are 12 layers of the walls and 12 gates in the city; and the height, length, and width are all the same—12,000 stadia (1,500 miles). The New Jerusalem is a perfect cube (although some scholarly commentators see it as a pyramid), the same shape as the holy of holies in the Temple (1 Kings 6:20). These measurements illustrate that this new home will be perfect for us, and the image portrays God as our Holy of Holies. All of the Holy City is the holy of holies, the whole city is the dwelling place of God; in the New Jerusalem God is as present in the streets as He was in the holy of holies in the Jerusalem of the past.

It is exciting to learn all that John has to tell about the measure of the New Jerusalem. But what does God's Word have to say to us about the measure of men and women that will live there?

Psalm 15 (NIV): *LORD, who may dwell in your sanctuary? Who may live on your holy hill? He whose walk is blameless and who does what is righteous, who speaks the truth from his heart and has no slander on his tongue, who does his neighbor no wrong and casts no slur on his fellowman, who despises a vile man but honors those who fear the Lord, who keeps his oath even when it hurts, who lends his money without usury [to one of his own people—*AMP.] *and does not accept a bribe against the innocent. He who does these things will never be shaken.*

This psalm helps us examine our walk, our works, and our words (verse 2). Then we consider our relationship with others (verses 3-4), how we keep our promises and how we use our money (verse 5). Meditating on this psalm and pondering these standards, we can determine how we are coping as we live among sinful people whose standards and morals are eroding. Our standards for living should not come from our evil society but from God. We must correct any tendency to neglect obeying God's Word and determine to deepen our relationship with Him.

Another passage that speaks to the measure of men and women was spoken by Jesus in Mark 12:29-31, *The most important one [commandment] . . . is this: . . . "Love the Lord your God with all your heart and with all your soul and with all your mind and with all your strength." The second is this: "Love your neighbor as yourself." There is no commandment greater than these* (NIV).

How are you measuring up to these passages?

MEMORY CHALLENGE

How do you serve Him?

Preparing a Place for Us

Read Revelation 21:18-21.

The vision of walls made of jasper with foundation stones adorned with precious stones reveals that the New Jerusalem will be a place of beauty, purity, and durability. It will last forever.

1. Describe the gates in the walls.

   Do you remember this chorus of this old hymn?

   > *He the pearly gates will open,*
   > *So that I may enter in;*
   > *For He purchased my redemption*
   > *And forgave me all my sin.**

2. What are the streets made of?

3. The Bible devotes less space to describing eternity than it does convincing people that eternal life is available as a free gift from God. Use phrases from the following passages to describe what we know about how eternity will be for us.

   John 14:2-3

   1 Corinthians 2:9

   Philippians 3:20-21

   1 John 3:2

   Revelation 21:1

Revelation 21:3

Revelation 21:4

Revelation 21:23

In heaven God is pictured as a Bridegroom whose Bride, the New Jerusalem, is adorned with jewels. The walls of the new Jerusalem are pictured as built of jasper, adorned with 12 kinds of jewels. Each of the 12 gates is made of a single pearl. The gems of the Holy City, like those in so much jewelry, are to be put in a setting of gold. The idea of rebuilding Jerusalem with jewels as building material fulfills Isaiah 54:11-12 (NIV), *O afflicted city, lashed by storms and not comforted, I will build you with stones of turquoise, your foundations with sapphires. I will make your battlements of rubies, your gates of sparkling jewels, and all your walls of precious stones.*

Solomon in all of his glory (1 Kings 10; 2 Chronicles 9) never knew, nor could he even have imagined, such splendor. John is attempting to convey through the limitations of human experience and language the incredible, unspeakable, magnificent wealth and beauty of heaven. It is unfathomable, beyond anything we can even imagine.

Precious stones are desirable because of rarity, hardness, and beauty. Their beauty is determined by color, transparency, luster, and brilliance. The Bible has three main lists of precious stones: the 12 stones of Aaron's breastplate (Exodus 28:17-20; 39:10-13), the treasures of the king of Tyre (Ezekiel 28:13), and those in our lesson today, the foundation stones of the New Jerusalem.

Gold is valued and used because of its rarity, beauty, and workability. It can be melted without harm and is easily molded. It can be used for cast objects, inlays, or overlays. A number of Israel's worship objects were solid gold or gilded (Exodus 37). Gold occurs in the Bible more frequently than any other metal, being used for jewelry (Exodus 12:35; 1 Timothy 2:9), idols, scepters, worship utensils, and money (Matthew 10:9; Acts 3:6). In addition, today's passage (Revelation 21:18) describes the New Jerusalem as made of gold.

The New Testament does not make much mention of jewels and jewelry. Pearls were highly valued in New Testament times and a fitting reference for the kingdom of God in Matthew 13:45-46: *The kingdom of heaven is like a merchant seeking fine pearls, and upon finding one pearl of great value, he went and sold all that he had and bought it.*

James warned his readers not to discriminate on the basis of wealth, as indicated by the wearing of gold rings (James 2:1-7). *What will it profit a man if he gains the whole world and forfeits his soul?* (Matthew 16:26).

How blessed is the man who finds wisdom and the man who gains understanding. For her profit is better than the profit of silver and her gain better than fine gold. She is more precious than jewels; and nothing you desire compares with her (Proverbs 3:13-15).

Tourists pay millions of dollars annually to tour mansions and castles to admire collections of antiques, art, and jewels. Heaven is all of this and more too. Jesus has gone there to prepare a place just for _____ (your name). It will all be yours to enjoy, including fellowship with the Father. What is the admission price? It is a free gift from God through His Son Jesus.

> We read of a place that's called Heaven,
>   It's made for the pure and the free;
> These truths in God's Word He hath given,
>   How beautiful Heaven must be.
>
> In Heaven no drooping nor pining,
> No wishing for elsewhere to be;
> God's light is forever there shining,
>   How beautiful Heaven must be.
>
> Pure waters of life there are flowing,
>   And all who will drink may be free;
> Rare jewels of splendor are glowing,
>   How beautiful Heaven must be.
>
> How beautiful Heaven must be,
>   Sweet home of the happy and free;
> Fair haven of rest for the weary,
>   How beautiful Heaven must be.**

*"He the Pearly Gates Will Open," Fred Blom, 1867-1927.

**"How Beautiful Heaven Must Be," A. S. Bridgewater, 20th century; A. P. Bland, 20th century.

MEMORY CHALLENGE

Why do we serve Him?

DAY SIX

The Light of God

Read Revelation 21:22-27.

1. Describe the temple of the Holy City.

2. Summarize verse 23.

3. What phrase in 1 John 1:5 confirms this?

4. What is explained about the gates in Revelation 21:25?

5. Who will be allowed entrance into the Holy City?

At the heart of Jewish life and faith was the Temple in Jerusalem. Before that was the Tabernacle in the wilderness with Moses. The Tabernacle and the Temple were provided as a meeting place of God with humanity—a place to draw near to God and to worship Him. But in the New Jerusalem there is no Temple. Why not? In heaven, God is the temple! Heaven is a place of constant intimacy with Him with continuous worship of Him. His eternal presence makes the whole city a sanctuary.

The city of God needs no created light. Isaiah 60:19-20 tells us: *No longer will you have the sun for light by day, nor for brightness will the moon give you light; but you will have the LORD for an everlasting light, and your God for your glory. Your sun will no longer set, nor will your moon wane; for you will have the LORD for an everlasting light, and the days of your mourning will be over.*

Psalm 36:9 says, *In Your light we see light.*

Heaven is always bright and beautiful—no gloomy days or depressing weather. The bright light of God radiates all around.

Revelation 21:24, 26 says, *The kings of the earth will bring their glory into it . . . and they will bring the glory and the honor of the nations into it.*

John envisions God as bringing all nations, including the Gentiles, into the Holy City. He sees all nations coming to God and all kings bringing their gifts and their honor. In other words, here is a picture of universal salvation, offered to all the world, the picture of a world for God. All good thoughts, good words, and good deeds will be gathered up and made a part of God's city.

Zechariah 2:11 tells us, *Many nations will join themselves to the LORD in that day and will become My people. Then I will dwell in your midst, and you will know that the LORD of hosts has sent Me to you.*

There will never be night there because it is lit continually by the glory of God. The gates will never be shut because there is no night there and no need for protection. The kings of the earth will bring their glory in, not to compete with the glory of God, but to have it revealed by the light of God. Nothing impure will enter because only the redeemed are admitted.

It is exciting to look forward to being in heaven, but until that time comes we must *be patient and stand firm, because the Lord's coming is near* (James 5:8, NIV).

"This little light of mine, I'm gonna let it shine. This little light of mine, I'm gonna let it shine, Let it shine, Let it shine, Let it shine." Does your light shine? Second Corinthians 3:18 (TLB) says, *We Christians . . . can be mirrors that brightly reflect the glory of the Lord. And as the Spirit of the Lord works within us, we become more and more like him.* Do you reflect Jesus, or is there a shadow between you and God?

How can we be *mirrors that brightly reflect the glory of the Lord?* What is glory? It is hard to define words like *glory, radiance, majesty.* The Jews saw the glory of God as the visible evidence of an invisible person. *The Son is the radiance of God's glory* (Hebrews 1:3, NIV).

Jesus Christ is the visible evidence of the invisible God. Therefore, through Him, we can understand the unknowable, experience the spiritual, feel the intangible, and see the invisible. Jesus' works glorified the Father and reflected His will in daily living for all to see. *The glory which You have given Me I have given to them* (John 17:22).

How do we become a reflector? Do all your work to the glory of God!
(1) Personally: *Have no other gods before Me* (Exodus 20:3). There are great benefits in this—peace, order, spiritual freedom, guidance for life.
(2) In family: As we treat each family member as God prescribes, we are reflecting God in our homes. For example: *Husbands, love your wives* (Ephesians 5:25). *Teach . . . your children* (Deuteronomy 6:7, RSV).

(3) In our daily workplace: *Whatever you do, do your work heartily, as for the Lord* (Colossians 3:23). We are not working for bosses, corporations, or companies, but for the Lord. Therefore, we must honor Him in our work. Others will see our diligence, honesty, and joy.

(4) In personal relationships: Choose friends wisely. *He who walks with wise men will be wise, but the companion of fools will suffer harm* (Proverbs 13:20).

(5) In financial management: *Store up . . . treasures in heaven* (Matthew 6:20). God does not need our money, but He wants our hearts, which are reflected by our giving.

(6) In problems: *Call on Me in the day of trouble; I shall rescue you, and you will honor Me* (Psalm 50:15). Let God be glorified in your problems. He wants to be your Source, not your last resort.

How do I know when I am not a reflector of God? Suggested indicators:

(1) Worry: evidence that we are competing with God about what we should do. *Cast all your anxiety on him* (1 Peter 5:7, NIV).

(2) Fear: What are you afraid of? *The LORD is my light and my salvation; whom shall I fear? The LORD is the defense of my life; whom shall I dread?* (Psalm 27:1). From this verse we see that light dispels the anxieties and dangers of darkness; salvation guarantees the defeat of all adversaries sent by Satan; defense (stronghold) assures victory against all evil assaults.

(3) Negativity: complaining, murmuring, and grumbling are all indications of not trusting God.

> Lamentations 3:39-42 tells us that complaining is a form of rebellion.
> 1 Samuel 15:23: *Rebellion is as the sin of witchcraft* (KJV); *divination* (NASB).
> Galatians 5:21: *Those who practice such things will not inherit the kingdom of God.*
> Philippians 2:14: *Do all things without grumbling.*
> Exodus 16:8: *Your grumblings are not against us but against the LORD.*

(4) Guilt: real or imagined. Confess all sin and receive total forgiveness (1 John 1:9). Carrying guilt does not allow the glory of God to be reflected from you.

(5) Not remaining faithful in obedience to the small matters each day. We must live moment by moment, giving each moment to Him, seeking guidance, counsel, and blessing on each one. We must be ready to obey at all times. He wants us to be at peace and live in joy. When we continue in disobedience, we become less and less capable of seeing God and being a witness of His light.

(6) An unteachable spirit: The best teacher on earth cannot teach the person who thinks he or she knows it all already and who does not wish to learn. God gave us free choice, and if we insist on choosing our own way, we cannot learn His.

When we see Jesus from a pure heart, we become more and more like Him. If we continually look at Him, His image or reflection radiates from us. If we purpose to study deeply the truths of God and diligently incorporate them into our lives daily, we will become *mirrors that brightly reflect the glory of the Lord.*

Those who will not lay aside the evil of their ways are barred from the city of God. It is not every sinner who is barred; Christ Jesus came into the world to save sinners. The person who is barred is the one who deliberately continues to sin; the one who, knowing Christ's way and the offer of Christ's grace available to him, still refuses the grace that could cleanse his or her sins. There is a sinner who hates his or her sin; and there is a sinner who loves his or her sin. There are those who sin against their will; there are sinners who choose to sin. It is not the repentant sinner, but the defiant sinner, who is barred from the city of God.

Written by Marie Coody

MEMORY CHALLENGE

Write the entire verse for today.

Revelation

LESSON 22

■ A Study of Revelation 22

DAY ONE

Paradise Restored

Read Revelation 22, concentrating on verses 1-2.

1. Describe the river in the New Jerusalem.

2. What does a river represent in these passages?

   Psalm 1:1-3

   Isaiah 33:21

   Isaiah 66:12

   John 7:38

3. List three differences in the tree of life in the new Jerusalem from the fruit trees of today.

4. From Ezekiel 47:12 describe a similar vision where waters flowed from the Temple.

5. What are the similarities in Genesis 2:8-10 when paradise was created and Revelation 22:1-2 when paradise was restored?

6. What else would your personal paradise include?

We are entering the city today. We have been exploring the walls, gates, and foundations of the exterior of the Holy City; but now the scene moves to the interior.

Rivers appear often in Scripture. The Euphrates, the Nile, and the Jordan are actual rivers that have historical significance throughout the Bible. There are also symbolic rivers. In the vision of Ezekiel 47, the river flowed from the Temple and freshened the Dead Sea. Now at the end of the Book of Revelation, we read about the life-giving river that flows through the city. It flows from the throne of God and the Lamb. Earlier in the Book of Revelation, it had been promised that the Lamb would guide the martyrs *to*

MEMORY CHALLENGE

Psalm 103:22

Bless the LORD, all you works of His, in all places of His dominion; bless the LORD, O my soul!

springs of the water of life (7:17), which God affirmed from the throne (21:6). Now the river of the water of life is seen as it flows from the throne.

We first learned of the tree of life when paradise was created in the Garden of Eden. The tree of life was placed in the midst of the garden. It became an important consideration only after Adam and Eve disobeyed. Sin interrupted the quality of life God intended for them. They were to obey God (Genesis 2:17) in a family setting (verses 18-25) and perform their assigned tasks (verse 15). They had access to all the trees in the garden, including the tree of life, but God gave an explicit command not to eat of the tree of knowledge. Their relationship to God changed radically when they disobeyed that command. One of the radical changes was that they no longer had access to the tree of life (3:22-24) because they could not have eternal life as long as they were under sin's control. Those who eat from the fruit of this tree will live forever. If Jesus has forgiven your sins, you will have the right to eat from the tree of life.

As paradise is restored, the abundant life God gives to His people is there for the taking. God will create trees that will produce fruit in every month; and the one who eats from them will be healed. Only by the power of God will the wounds and disagreements of the nations be healed.

The biblical account of human life began with a garden. It ends with a city. But the city is to have all the characteristics of the garden. We can eat of the tree and drink of the river and walk with Him *in the cool of the day* (Genesis 3:8).

DAY TWO

Life in Heaven

Read Revelation 22:3-5.

1. *And there will no longer be a curse.* Record the promise that is fulfilled with this part of the vision (Zechariah 14:11).

2. Who is with God on the throne?

3. Looking back to Revelation 7:14-15, explain who the bondservants are.

4. What is required in order to be allowed to see His face and have His name on your forehead?

   Psalm 17:15

   Matthew 5:8

   Hebrews 12:14

5. How long is the reign of His victorious servants?

6. How do you picture your life in heaven?

7. Psalm 24:3 asks, *Who may ascend into the hill of the LORD? and who may stand in His holy place?* Record Psalm 24:4-5 for the answer.

And there will no longer be a curse. There will be only pure life and blessing. Every effect of God's displeasure for sin is now totally removed. In the heavenly city the Christian, after all the battles on earth, will have nothing to tempt him or her from the purity sought on earth.

There are some biblical teachings that help us understand evil and curses from the Christian perspective:

(1) God limited himself by giving humankind freedom. To live in freedom, a person must have the power of choice.

(2) Humans need freedom of choice even with the possibility of bringing evil into the world. The Bible tells us that with the Fall, humanity's first sin, a radical change took place in the universe. Death came upon humankind (Genesis 2:17; 3:2-3, 19). God pronounced a curse upon humankind:

> Anguish in childbearing (3:16)
> Male domination over wife (3:16)
> Toilsome labor (3:17)
> Thorns and thistles (3:18)

These are probably only a sample of the actual effects upon creation. In Romans 8:22, Paul said that the whole creation has been affected by human sin and is now in bondage to decay.

(3) Behind the disobedience of Adam and Eve was Satan. In Genesis 3 we read that the serpent tempted Eve. Thus, an evil force was present within the creation. It was Satan's appeal that led them to sin. (Compare with Revelation 12:9.) It is clear, then, that God did not create evil and sin that resulted in curses. He merely provided the options necessary for human freedom.

(4) Even though evil is caused by human disobedience and failure, God actively continues to redeem people from their self-imposed evil with His willingness to forgive.

(5) God deals with evil through judgment and wrath. This judgment can be seen in the Old Testament (Deuteronomy 28:20-21; Isaiah 3:11). The wrath of God is not divine vindictiveness but a dynamic, persistent opposition to sin (Romans 1:18).

(6) God deals with evil through the Incarnation, the Cross, and the Resurrection. The Bible teaches that God himself in Jesus Christ became the victim of evil so that there might be victory over evil. It is His victory over evil (Satan) that allows man to enter into the presence of the living God—into the Holy City.

Thankfully, none of this evil will mar the beautiful life of heaven where we observe the bondservants serving God and the Lamb. There is nothing that they would rather do; there is no greater pleasure or joy than the service of God. At last in His service they will find perfect freedom, and in perfect submission to Him they will find the only true royalty. They will have intimate fellowship with Him. They will see His face and have His name on their foreheads. And they shall have authority—they shall reign forever and ever.

Do you think heaven will be boring? No, boredom is a sign of selfishness. You want someone to do something for you; you want some excitement to be brought into your life. But all selfishness will be ended; therefore, there will be no boredom in heaven. There is continual excitement, discovery, anticipation—and constant gratitude and praise.

MEMORY CHALLENGE

Fill in the blanks:

Bless the _____, all you _____ of His,

in all places of His _____; bless the

LORD, O _____ _____!

> Psalm 103:22

Jesus Will Return

Read Revelation 22:6-9.

1. In this passage we have three speakers. The first to speak is one of the angels who has been the interpreter of the vision to John. He explains that the messages, the words, and the visions that came to John are from the same God who inspired the great prophets of the Old Testament. *These words are* _____ *and* _____.

2. The second speaker is Jesus Christ himself. What is His message?

   How can a person *heed the words* of the prophecy of this book?

3. What do these scriptures teach us about the second coming of Jesus (the Apocalypse)?

   Matthew 24:42

   Matthew 24:44

   Mark 13:32

   Mark 13:35-37

   1 Thessalonians 5:1-2

   Revelation 3:3

John, the last speaker, warns us, as he did in earlier chapters, that the worship of angels is wrong and that worship must be given to God and to God alone.

4. In what way do we put Christian leaders on pedestals or revere them too highly?

   How can we put believers we respect in proper perspective?

5. How have you been influenced by those who give specific dates for the return of Christ?

   What do we know about the timing of Christ's return?

First-century Christians were not exhorted to discover the date of the world's end but instead were instructed to keep their *eyes on Jesus, the author and perfecter of [their] faith* (Hebrews 12:2). All of the biblical passages admonishing Christians to expectantly look for their Savior's return were written to help believers fix their hearts on God rather than on the earthly attachments of life, which are insignificant in comparison to the heavenly awards that await them at Jesus' second coming.

There is certainly nothing wrong with Christians looking forward to the return of their Lord and Savior. The apostles Paul and John both prayed for Jesus to come back (1 Corinthians 16:22; Revelation 22:20). Such a sincere desire gives comfort and hope to individuals living in a decidedly difficult world full of complex problems. But no one has ever benefited from the disappointment and embarrassment linked to failed prophecies, predictions, and suggestions about "the end time."

Today's Christian would be wiser to spend fewer hours studying prophecy books filled with unproven conjectures and more hours studying the depth of biblical passages relating to love, kindness, self-control, patience, thoughtfulness, and forgiveness. According to God's Word, the timing of Jesus' second appearance is not nearly as important as the events that took place during His first appearance— His death and resurrection.

MEMORY CHALLENGE

Where are we to bless the Lord?

Almost Persuaded

Read Revelation 22:10-11.

1. Why was John instructed not to seal the prophecy of his vision?

2. In Daniel 8:26, how was Daniel instructed concerning his vision?

3. Why do you think the angel tells everyone to continue doing what he or she is doing, whether good or bad? (Hint: Ezekiel 3:27.)

4. Summarize Matthew 12:32, which deals with the unpardonable sin.

John believed that the return of Christ could happen any moment. This was not a time to record and file away the prophecy of his vision. Believing that, what is the meaning of the passage that seems to say that people must remain as they are?

There comes a time when a person can be so set in character that all any situation can do is to make him or her more deeply and more permanently what he or she is. It is the greatest human tragedy—a person can so long refuse the way of Christ that in the end he or she cannot change to accept it. Can this be the sin against the Holy Spirit, the unpardonable sin?

An ancient commentator, Andreas, explains that, in effect, Jesus is saying, "Let each man do what pleases him; I will not force a choice. I use no compulsion; the only weapon I use is appeal; as a man chooses to make himself, so let him be; for only if he allows me to can I remake him." This, then, would be another warning that every person is writing his or her own destiny.

John is giving us another reminder that each day we are

working out one of two destinies. Either we are following the Lord, walking with Him and doing right or, by not making a choice to be His, we have already chosen the way of evil. There is no escape except the way of faith in Christ. You will have to continue in the way you are going.

> *Church is finally over, I'm headed for the door.*
> *The sermon was inspiring like hundreds were before.*
> *The choir sang the anthem the best I've ever heard,*
> *And all the people list'ning were blessed and even stirred.*
> *The invitation given was earnest, warm and strong*
> *While all the congregation joined in the final song.*
> *I almost was persuaded to let the Savior in*
> *But church is finally over, I turned away again.*
> *Church is finally over, I feel about the same.*
> *I guess I'll wait 'til next time to call upon His name.*
> *They say He is very patient, long suffering and kind*
> *His arms are always open and those who seek shall find.*
> *I've heard the gospel story until I know it well*
> *How Jesus died to save me from everlasting hell.*
> *Yet I can't help but wonder when my last chance will be*
> *And church is finally over for all eternity.**

*Copyright 1968 by Lexicon Music, Inc. Words and music to "Church Is Finally Over" by Ralph Carmichael. Used by permission.

God's Word gives strong warnings to those who do not choose salvation through Jesus Christ:

Proverbs 1:20-32: *Wisdom shouts in the street, she lifts her voice in the square; at the head of the noisy streets she cries out; at the entrance of the gates in the city, she utters her sayings: "How long, O naive ones, will you love being simple-minded? And scoffers delight themselves in scoffing and fools hate knowledge? Turn to my reproof, behold, I will pour out my spirit on you; I will make my words known to you. Because I called and you refused, I stretched out my hand and no one paid attention; and you neglected all my counsel and did not want my reproof; I will also laugh at your calamity; I will mock when your dread comes, when your dread comes like a storm and your calamity comes on like a whirlwind, when distress and anguish come on you. Then they will call on me, but I will not answer; they will seek me diligently but they will not find me, because they hated knowledge and did not choose the fear of the LORD. They would not accept my counsel, they spurned all my reproof. So they shall eat of the fruit of their own way and be satiated with their own devices. For the waywardness of the naive will kill them, and the complacency of fools will destroy them."*

Proverbs 6:15: *Therefore his [the wicked man's] calamity will come suddenly; instantly he will be broken and there will be no healing.*

Dear God, thank You for Your loving warnings and the faithfulness of the Holy Spirit to shed light on any area of our lives that needs correction.

MEMORY CHALLENGE

Fill in the blanks:

Bless the LORD, *all you works of His, in* _____

_____ *of* _____ _____;

bless the LORD, _____ _____ _____*!*

Psalm 103:22

Oh, What a Day!

Read Revelation 22:12-21.

1. How is Jesus returning?

2. What is He bringing with Him?

3. Who will be entitled to citizenship in the new Jerusalem?

4. What is the consequence of living a life of disobedience to God?

5. What was Jesus' method for getting His message to us?

6. Do the self-descriptions of Jesus in this passage change the way you view Him?

In this last chapter of the Bible, John repeatedly states that Jesus is coming soon. In various ways he relates that you will be ready if you accept His call to holy living; you must be morally clean, forgiven, and washed in the blood of the Lamb.

"Come now, and let us reason together," says the LORD, *"though your sins are as scarlet, they will be as white as snow; though they are red like crimson, they will be like wool"* (Isaiah 1:18). This defies human logic, but it is God's way. We must believe it and live a godly life to be ready for Christ's return. Those who enter the city of God are those who have accepted and appropriated the sacrifice of Jesus Christ. The terms of the invitation (Revelation 22:17) are quite simple. If you are thirsty—really desire Christ, His